Challenges and Prospects for Clinical Trials in India

TEAM LEADER

Ali Mehdi established and leads the Health Policy Initiative at ICRIER. His research interests include—the process, design and assessment of health policies; prevention of chronic diseases along with policy instruments and institutional design for its promotion; social determinants of health; metrics of health inequities; health financing, governance and manpower; fertility and mortality; demographic dividend; drug regulation. A couple of his books are in the pipeline—*India Health Report 2018* (Oxford University Press), *A Shot of Justice* (2 volumes) (Oxford University Press), *Chronic Diseases in South Asia* (Springer), *Freedoms and Fragility: The Challenge of Job Creation in Kashmir, India* (Routledge). Ali did his MA at the University of Freiburg, Germany and completed his PhD at Humboldt University in Berlin. He can be reached at *amehdi@icrier.res.in*.

AUTHORS

Rahul Mongia is a Consultant at ICRIER, and a research scholar at the Centre for Studies in Science Policy (CSSP), Jawaharlal Nehru University. He has been working on issues related to the biopharmaceutical industry and health policy broadly. He has contributed to opinion columns in several national dailies and blogs. His research interests include intellectual property, technology transfers, FDI, trade negotiations, universal health coverage and issues related to the pharmaceutical product supply chain and drug development.

Deepmala Pokhriyal is a Consultant at ICRIER. She has worked on the assessment of the regulations of the clinical trials industry in India, and recommending potential changes based on the industry's global environment. She is also a graduate student at the Andrew Young School of Policy Studies, Georgia State University. Prior to this, she was engaged in a NABARD-sponsored project on evaluation of rural connectivity projects in Gujarat at Indian Institute of Management, Ahmedabad. She holds a graduate degree in Economics from Gokhale Institute of Politics and Economics, Pune.

Seema Rao is an External-Consultant at ICRIER. She is a practicing advocate in the Supreme Court of India and Delhi High Court. She has been a Panel lawyer for the Government in the Supreme Court as well as Standing Counsel on behalf of Ministry of Environment and Forest in the National Green Tribunal. During this time she dealt with matters relating to key policy making issues in environment laws, company laws, criminal laws, PILs etc. She has various national and international publications to her credit on topics relating to criminal laws, banking, environment laws etc.

Challenges and Prospects for Clinical Trials in India

A Regulatory Perspective

Team Leader
Ali Mehdi

Authors
Rahul Mongia
Deepmala Pokhriyal
Seema Rao

ACADEMIC FOUNDATION
NEW DELHI

www.academicfoundation.org

First published in 2017
by

ACADEMIC FOUNDATION
4772-73 / 23 Bharat Ram Road, (23 Ansari Road),
Darya Ganj, New Delhi - 110 002 (India).
Phones : 23245001 / 02.
Fax : +91-11-23245005.
E-mail : booksaf@gmail.com
www.academicfoundation.org

and

**INDIAN COUNCIL FOR RESEARCH ON INTERNATIONAL
ECONOMIC RELATIONS (ICRIER)**
Core 6A, 4th Floor India Habitat Centre, Lodhi Road, New Delhi 110003

© 2017
Copyright: ICRIER.

ALL RIGHTS RESERVED.
No part of this book shall be reproduced, stored in a retrieval system,
or transmitted by any means, electronic, mechanical, photocopying,
recording, or otherwise, without the prior written permission of the
copyright holder(s) and/or the publishers.

Disclaimer: Opinions and recommendations in the report are exclusively of the author(s) and not of any other individual or institution including ICRIER. This report has been prepared in good faith on the basis of information available at the date of publication. All interactions and transactions with industry sponsors and their representatives have been transparent and conducted in an open, honest and independent manner as enshrined in ICRIER Memorandum of Association. ICRIER does not accept any corporate funding that comes with a mandated research area which is not in line with ICRIER's research agenda. The corporate funding of an ICRIER activity does not, in any way, imply ICRIER's endorsement of the views of the sponsoring organization or its products or policies. ICRIER does not conduct research that is focused on any specific product or service provided by the corporate sponsor.

Citation:
Mongia, R., Pokhriyal, D., Rao, S., Mehdi, A.* (2017). *Challenges and prospects for clinical trials in India: A regulatory perspective.* New Delhi: Academic Foundation.

(*: Corresponding Author: *amehdi@icrier.res.in*)

Cataloging in Publication Data–DK
 Courtesy: D.K. Agencies (P) Ltd. <docinfo@dkagencies.com>

Mehdi, Ali, author.
   Challenges and prospects for clinical trials in India : a regulatory perspective.
    pages cm
  Includes bibliographical references.
  ISBN 9789332704268

   1. Clinical trials–Law and legislation–India.   I. Mongia, Rahul, author. II. Pokhriyal, Deepmala, author. III. Rao, Seema (Advocate), author. IV. Indian Council for Research on International Economic Relations, issuing body. V. Title.

KNS1520.M44 2017   DDC 344.54041   23

Typeset, printed and bound by The Book Mint, New Delhi.
www.thebookmint.in

Contents

List of Tables, Figures and Appendices 7
List of Abbreviations 8
Glossary 10
Foreword 12
Acknowledgements 14
Executive Summary 16

1. **Introduction** 18
   1.1 Regulating Clinical Research
   1.2 The Global Clinical Research Landscape
   1.3 The Indian Clinical Research Growth Story

2. **Research Methodology** 26
   2.1 Country Selection Criteria

3. **The Dilemmas Afflicting Clinical Research in India** 30
   3.1 Overview
   3.2 Developing a Culture of Research and Innovation:
        The Clinical Research Perspective
   3.3 Regulatory Landscape for Clinical Research of Countries in the Sample

4. **Under Trial: The Challenge of Clinical Trials in India** 40
   4.1 Use of Formulae for Calculating Compensation
        for Trial Related Injury/Death
   4.2 Use of a 'Standard of Care'
   4.3 Use of Placebos in a Placebo Controlled Trial
   4.4 Clinical Trial Waivers
   4.5 Mandatory Local Filing of Marketing Authorisation After the Clinical Trial
   4.6 Audio-visual Recording of Informed Consent
   4.7 Message Fidelity in Translated Informed Consent Forms
   4.8 Trends in Clinical Research in Other Countries
   4.9 Policy Recommendations

5. Conclusions 70

References. 72
Appendices 74

List of Tables, Figures and Appendices

Tables

1.1 Contribution of Select Countries to Clinical Research (CTs Registered) 21

2.1 Country/Region Selection Criteria 27

2.2 Cross-section of Respondents across Disciplines and Occupations 28

3.1 Comparison of Phase 3 Global Clinical Trials vs Local Clinical Trials 33

3.2 SAEs (Death) Reported During the Period of 2005 to 2016. 36

3.3 SAEs (Injury) Reported During the Period of 2005 to 2016. 37

3.4 Clinical Trial Committee Classification of the Review of CTAs in South Africa 50

4.1 Table Depicting Criteria for Compensation for Trial Related Injury/Death. 62

Figures

1.1 Clinical Trials Phases: A Quick Primer 22

1.2 Relative Number versus Percentual Substitution Per Region in 2006 and 2012 . . 22

1.3 Growth of Global Clinical Trials in India: 2000 and 2015 24

2.1 Algorithm Followed for Screening Records in CTRI Database. 28

3.1 Registered Clinical Trial in India: Trial Type Profile. 32

3.2 Registered Clinical Trials in India: Intervention Type Profile 32

3.3 Registered Clinical Trials in India: Sponsor Profile. 33

3.4 Registered Clinical Trials: Sponsor-site Profile 34

3.5 Registered Clinical Trials in India: Phase Profile 34

3.6 An Overview of the Drug Development Process 40

3.7 Registered Trials in India: Disease Category-Sponsor Profile 41

Appendices

I Registered Ethics Committees in India (State-wise). 75

II Causality between Intervention and Injury/Death. 76

III Clinical Trial Registries and their Evolution 79

IV Snapshot of Country wise Regulations and Field Findings 82

V The Swasthya Adhikar Manch & Others Vs Union of India: A Timeline. 83

VI Schematic Diagram of Review Process of Clinical Trial Application in India 85

VII Timeline of Changes in Regulation from 2013 to Till Date 86

List of Abbreviations

AAHRR	Association for the Accreditation of Human Research Protection Programs, Inc.
ABPI	Association of the British Pharmaceutical Industry
ADR	Adverse Drug Reaction
AE	Adverse Events
AIDS	Acquired Immune Deficiency Syndrome
AMA	American Medical Association
API	Active Pharmaceutical Ingredient
AYUSH	Ayurveda, Yoga and Naturopathy, Unani, Siddha and Homoeopathy
BA/BE	Bioavailibility/Bioequivalence
BfArM	Federal Institute for Drugs and Medical Devices
CDSA	Clinical Development Services Agency
CDSCO	Central Drugs Standard Control Organization
CIOMS	Council for International Organization of Medical Sciences
COHRED	Council on Health Research for Development
CRO	Contract Research Organization
CT	Clinical Trial
CTA	Clinical Trial Application
CTC	Clinical Trial Committee
CTN	Clinical Trial Notification
CTRI	Clinical Trial Registry of India
CTU	Clinical Trial Unit
D&C Act	Drugs and Cosmetics Act, 1940
D&C Rules	Drugs and Cosmetic Rules, 1945
DCG (I)	Drug Controller General of India
DGHS	Directorate General of Health Services
DHHS	Department of Health and Human Services
DTAB	Drugs Technical Advisory Board
EC	Ethics Committee
EU	European Union
EVCTM	EudraVigilance Clinical Trial Module
FDC	Fixed Dose Combination
FERCAP	Forum for Ethics Review Committees in Asia Pacific
FERCI	Forum for Ethics Review Committees in India
FIBCO	Fully Integrated Biopharmaceutical Company
FIPCO	Fully Integrated Pharmaceutical Company
GATT	General Agreement on Tariffs and Trade
GCP	Good Clinical Practices
GCT	Global Clinical Trial
GRMRSA	General Regulations Made in Terms of the Medicines and Related Substances Act
HIV	Human Immunodeficiency Virus
HMSC	Health Ministry's Screening Committee
HSA	Health Sciences Authority

ICF	Informed Consent Form	NIH	National Institutes of Health
ICH	International Council on Harmonisation of Technical Requirements for Registration of Pharmaceuticals for Human Use	NIHRD	National Institute of Health Research and Development
		NRES	National Research Ethics Service
ICMR	Indian Council for Medical Research	OHRP	Office for Human Research Protections
ICSR	Individual Case Safety Report	PRISMA	Preferred Reporting Items for Systematic Reviews and Meta-Analyses
ICTRP	WHO International Clinical Trials Registry Platform		
		QCI	Quality Council of India
IMP	Investigational Medicinal Product	R&D	Research and Development
IND	Investigational New Drug	RCT	Randomised Control Trials
IRB	Institutional Review Board	SADAG	South African Depression & Anxiety Group
MCC	Medicines Control Council		
MHRA	Medicines and Healthcare Products Regulatory Agency	SADR	Serious Adverse Drug Reaction
		SAE	Serious Adverse Event
MoHFW	Ministry of Health and Family Welfare	SANCTR	South African National Clinical Trials Register
MRCT	Multi Regional Clinical Trials	SEC	Subject Expert Committee
NABH	National Accreditation Board for Hospitals & Healthcare Providers	SIDCER	Strategic Initiative for Developing Capacity in Ethical Review
NADFC	National Agency of Drug and Food Control	TGA	Therapeutic Goods Administration
		TRC	Technical Review Committee
NCD	Non-Communicable Diseases	TRIPS	Trade-Related Aspects of Intellectual Property Rights
NCE	New Chemical Entity		
NDA	New Drug Application	UMC	Uppsala Monitoring Centre
NDAC	New Drugs Advisory Committee	USFDA	United States Food and Drug Administration
NDRA	National Drug Regulatory Authority		
		WHO	World Health Organization
NHREC	National Health Research Ethics Council	WMA	World Medical Association

Glossary

Adverse Drug Reaction (ADR)	(a) In case of approved pharmaceutical products: A noxious and unintended response at doses normally used or tested in humans
	(b) In case of new unregistered pharmaceutical products (or those products which are not yet approved for the medical condition where they are being tested): A noxious and unintended response at any dose(s)
	The phrase ADR differs from Adverse Event (AE), in case of an ADR there appears to be a reasonable possibility that the AE is related with the medicinal product being studied. In clinical trials, an untoward medical occurrence seemingly caused by overdosing, abuse/dependence and interactions with other medicinal products is also considered as an ADR.
Adverse Event (AE)	Any untoward medical occurrence (including a symptom/disease or an abnormal laboratory finding) during treatment with a pharmaceutical product in a patient or a human volunteer that does not necessarily have a relationship with the treatment being given.
Biopharmaceutical	Any compound composed of DNA, RNA, or protein. For example: recombinant proteins (rDNA), monoclonal antibodies (mAbs), biologics from natural sources and antisense oligonucleotides. In this report for all practical purposes, a biopharmaceutical is treated as any entity that breaches the Lipinski Rule limit of molecular weight of 500D in order to differentiate it from small molecules.
Clinical Study	A systematic study of pharmaceutical products on human subjects—(whether patients or non-patient volunteers)—in order to discover or verify the clinical, pharmacological (including pharmacodynamics / pharmacokinetics), and/or adverse effects, with the object of determining their safety and/or efficacy.
Clinical Trial	A systematic study of any new drug(s) in human subject(s) to generate data for discovering and/or verifying the clinical, pharmacological (including pharmacodynamic and pharmacokinetic) and/or adverse effects with the objective of determining safety and/or efficacy of the new drug.
Comparator Product	A pharmaceutical product (including placebo) used as a reference in a clinical trial.
Contract Research Organisation (CRO)	An organisation to which the sponsor may transfer or delegate some or all of the tasks, duties and/or obligations regarding a Clinical Study. All such contractual transfers of obligations should be defined in writing. A CRO is a scientific body—commercial, academic or other.
Global Clinical Trial	Any clinical trial which is conducted as part of multi-national clinical development of a drug. These are concurrent trials unlike the phase lagged trials or the bridging studies.

Investigational Product	A pharmaceutical product (including the comparator product) being tested or used as reference in a clinical study. An investigational product may be an active chemical entity or a formulated dosage form.
Investigator	A researcher involved in a clinical trial and responsible for the scientific and technical direction of the entire clinical trial.
Investigational New Drug	A new chemical entity or a product having therapeutic indication but which has never been tested earlier on a human being.
New Chemical Entity	An active substance in developmental stage which may be specified as a drug under the D&C Act, after undergoing any clinical trial.
New Drug	A drug, including bulk drugs substance which has not been used in India to any significant extent under the conditions prescribed, recommended or suggested in its labeling and has not been recognised as effective and safe by the licensing authority for the proposed claims, drugs already approved for certain claims, which are now proposed to be marketed with modified or new claims (viz., new indications, dosage, dosage forms or routes of administration), or fixed dose combinations of two or more drugs, individually approved earlier for certain claims, which are now proposed to be combined for the first time in a fixed ratio, or a new fixed ratio, with certain claims, (viz., indications, dosage, dosage forms or routes of administration).
Pharmacodynamics	The study of biochemical and physiological effects of drugs on an organism and the relationship between drug concentration and effect, i.e. what a drug does to the body.
Pharmacokinetics	The analysis of the course of substances in the body and their relationship with an organism or system over time. A pharmacokinetic study is a systematic assessment of what the body does to a drug after it has been introduced into the body.
Pre-clinical	All research and development conducted prior to the initiation of clinical testing, including discovery, in vitro testing, and animal studies.
Serious Adverse Event (SAE)	An AE or ADR that is associated with death, inpatient hospitalisation (in case the study was being conducted on out-patients), prolongation of hospitalisation (in case the study was being conducted on in-patients), persistent or significant disability or incapacity, a congenital anomaly or birth defect, or is otherwise life threatening.
Sponsor	An individual or a company or an institution that takes the responsibility for the initiation, management and/or financing of a clinical study. An Investigator who independently initiates and takes full responsibility for a trial automatically assumes the role of a sponsor.

Foreword

Clinical trials are indispensable to the drug development process to ensure the efficacy and safety of any new drug—they are the mainstay for introducing newer and better therapeutics into any market. There is an urgent need for the growth of clinical trials in India considering that India is home to 16 per cent of the world population, has 20 per cent of the global disease burden but has less than 2 per cent of the clinical trials registered worldwide.

This report analyses prospects and challenges of clinical trials in India, focusing on New Chemical Entities (NCEs) and new drugs. It situates the debate around clinical research in the context of new drug approval process and attempts to gauge the impact of the regulatory changes brought about in the sphere of clinical research in India while conducting a perceptional analysis of stakeholders across the spectrum.

There are several actionable policy recommendations in this report that can be adopted to improve the conduct and quality of clinical trials so as to bring about transparency and fairness. This in turn will enable the pharmaceutical industry and clinical research organisations to contribute effectively to public health by conducting more clinical trials in India while addressing concerns raised regarding the conduct and quality.

I hope all stakeholders—particularly policymakers in the Government of India, representatives of pharmaceutical industry, civil society, international organisations and the academia—would find this report interesting and stimulating.

— Rajat Kathuria
Director and Chief Executive
Indian Council for Research on International Economic Relations (ICRIER)
New Delhi

Acknowledgements

Conducting the comprehensive and analytical nature of research that we have been under the Health Policy Initiative (HPI) at ICRIER since 2014 would not have been possible without the generous and unconditional financial support provided by the Pharmaceutical Research and Manufacturers of America (PhRMA), Washington DC. We would, therefore, like to, first and foremost, thank PhRMA in general and Ms Amiee Aloi, Deputy Vice President of International Advocacy at PhRMA in particular for such support—and more importantly, for an independent think-tank like ICRIER, their supportive attitude towards our nonpartisan approach.

As part of our nonpartisan approach, we, at HPI, adopted a strong stakeholder orientation from the beginning. All topics of research, and their scope, were decided based on discussions during two multistakeholder workshops in early 2014. Since then, we have maintained this orientation and we would like to thank all stakeholders, in India and abroad, who participated in this study and made it possible—during the course of various consultations, one-to-one meetings, etc.

We have been privileged to have some of the most renowned national and international experts in the field to review this study and offer their insightful comments for improvement. Mr Mark Barnes and Dr Barbara Bierer of the prestigious Multiregional Clinical Trials Center (MRCT) at Harvard University, USA; Mr Richard Kingham, Senior Counsel, Covington & Burling LLP in Washington, DC/London as well as Adjunct Professor at the Georgetown University Law Centre, USA; Ms Susan Winckler, President of Leavitt Partners Consulting, Washington, DC, USA; Dr Lembit Rago, Secretary General, Council for International Organizations of Medical Sciences (CIOMS), Geneva; Mr Andy Gray, Senior Lecturer, Division of Pharmacology, School of Health Sciences, University of KwaZulu-Natal, South Africa; Dr B.K. Rana, CEO Incharge, National Accreditation Board for Hospitals and Healthcare Providers (NABH), New Delhi; Dr Santanu Tripathi, Professor and Head, Department of Clinical and Experimental Pharmacology, Calcutta School of Tropical Medicine, Kolkata; Mr D.G. Shah, Secretary General of the Indian Pharmaceutical Alliance (IPA), Mumbai and Mr Ajay Sharma, Director (Research and Government Affairs), Organization of Pharmaceuticals Producers of India (OPPI), Mumbai; deserve special mention in this regard.

Our special thanks are due to highly distinguished members of the Advisory Committee of our Research Program on Drug Regulatory Reforms in India. We benefited immensely from their guidance and support throughout the process of this study. We would like to thank Richard and Susan in particular for travelling all the way from Washington, DC to participate in the Advisory Committee meetings.

Finally—and most importantly—I would like to express my profoundest gratitude to Dr Rajat Kathuria, Director and CE, ICRIER and my HPI colleagues who worked with great dedication and put out their best at various stages of this study. Two former members of HPI, Ms Arunima Wanchoo and Dr Joyita Chowdhury contributed to the study in various ways, and I would like to acknowledge and appreciate their work. All credit goes to the aforementioned, while I take responsibility for any shortcomings that remain.

This acknowledgement would not be complete without thanking Mr Sanu Kapila and Ms Sona Kapila at Academic Foundation for promptly agreeing, preparing and bringing out this report in such a professional manner. A big thank you to them and their team!

—Ali Mehdi
Fellow and Project Leader
Health Policy Initiative
Indian Council for Research on International Economic Relations (ICRIER), New Delhi
email: amehdi@icrier.res.in

Executive Summary

Executive Summary

Clinical trials (CTs) are integral to drug discovery and bringing out newer and better medicines into the market. With the growing burden of disease and evolution of the nation's pharmaceutical industry, the need for clinical trials in India has increased manifold.

India has had favourable prerequisites for conducting clinical research—a large and diverse patient pool, a highly skilled workforce of qualified scientists, medical colleges, etc. Yet, an unfavourable ecosystem has undermined its potential—only 19 trials were approved in 2013, a drop of roughly 93 per cent from 2012 (262 trials), and a fraction of its peak of 500 trials in 2010. India is home to 16 per cent of the world population and 20 per cent of the global burden of disease; yet, it has less than 2 per cent of clinical trials registered worldwide. A critical area of concern where the country continues to underperform despite enormous potential to be a world leader.

This report analyses prospects and challenges of clinical trials in India, focusing on New Chemical Entities (NCEs) and new drugs. It contextualises the debate around clinical research in the context of new drug approval process. Likewise, it proposes actionable policy recommendations for Indian drug regulatory landscape so that the country could realise its untapped potential while addressing concerns raised regarding the conduct and quality of clinical trials. The objective of drug regulation is both protection and promotion of public health. It is high time India's drug regulatory landscape delivers on both. Regulatory lacunas surrounding clinical trials have impacted promotion of public health severely—they need to be addressed promptly to bring about transparency and fairness so that the pharmaceutical industry and clinical research organisations can move ahead within a clear-cut framework of regulatory expectations and contribute to public health.

1 Introduction

> The ethical basis of all [medical] research is that information gained from one patient's experience should, where feasible, be used to help others and to reduce suffering.
>
> —British Medical Association

CTs are indispensable to the drug development process to ensure the efficacy and safety of new drugs. They are the mainstay for introducing newer and better therapeutics into the market. Although many countries have a robust set of guidelines/codes for regulating the conduct of CTs, their practice and implementation have been looked upon as areas of ethical and regulatory concerns respectively. India has had favourable prerequisites for conducting clinical research and drug development—a large and diverse patient pool (trial participants), a highly skilled workforce of qualified scientists (investigators), medical colleges (sites), etc. Yet, an unfavourable ecosystem has undermined its potential—only 19 trials were approved in 2013, a drop of roughly 93 per cent from 2012 (262 trials), and a fraction of its peak of 500 trials in 2010.[1] India is home to 16 per cent of world population and 20 per cent of the global disease burden, yet it has less than 2 per cent of CTs registered worldwide.[2] A critical area of concern where the country continues to underperform despite enormous potential to be a world leader.

While the pharmaceutical sector has registered higher growth vis-à-vis other sectors of the Indian economy, its clinical research industry has lagged behind (Mondal and Abrol 2015). Today, public opinion in India is not quite in favour of CTs as several contract research organisations (CROs) have been blamed for conducting trials without due concern for procedural and ethical issues.[3] Along with bad press and regulatory inadequacies, CTs almost came to a halt in India. This has had grave ramifications, from a counterfactual perspective, for public health due to delays in introducing new and relevant therapeutics, and may ultimately aggravate the problem of drug lag[4] in the country.

Looking into the history of regulation of randomised controlled trials (RCTs) across the globe, plugging regulatory gaps via codification of new principles and regulations[5] is a recurrent theme. India has followed a similar trend, and, of late, is attempting to plug the 'regulatory vacuum' by constituting expert committees—the (late) Ranjit Roy Chaudhary Committee being the most noted—to suggest reforms via amendments to existing law governing oversight of CTs and functioning of the National Drug Regulatory Authority (NDRA). The latest proposed amendment (now withdrawn) to the Drugs and Cosmetics Act, 1940 (henceforth, D&C Act) had several clauses that were either vague or contradicted existing rules under Schedule Y of the Drugs and Cosmetic Rules, 1945, (henceforth, D&C Rules). Key issues like that of 'compensation' to a trial participant for an injury in CTs to the scope of what constitutes an 'injury' have come into focus in this regard. Series of stakeholders, from sponsors of CTs to the investigators conducting CTs, have been left in the lurch because of the uncertainty prevailing in the system.[6]

On the other hand, there are long-standing issues like that of clinical/rational sense in medicinal products like combination drugs, whose use is supposedly rampant in India (Gautam and Saha 2007); questions like, what constitutes a 'new drug' and who provides for their approval (CDSCO or State Drug Regulatory Authorities) and the guidance/recommendations

---

1. See, http://cdsco.nic.in/writereaddata/DCG(I)%20approved%20clinical%20trial%20registered%20in%20ctri%20website%20(Jan.2013).pdf (Last accessed on 4 April 2017).
2. See, http://www.theweek.in/health/cover/clinical-trials-research-india.html (Last accessed on 4 April 2017).
3. See for instance, Parliamentary Committee 59th Report on The Functions of the Central Drug Standards Control Organisation (CDSCO).
4. A 'drug lag' refers to any delay in making a drug available in a particular market. However, it may also have positive externalities, if there is a danger of too-rapid introduction of medicines of unproven value. The term 'relevant therapeutics', hence, refers to a medicine that caters to the public health needs of a country.
5. From the thalidomide tragedy that triggered the Kefauver-Harris Drug Amendments, 1962 and the Investigational Drug Regulations in 1963 in US to the new EU regulations (EU Clinical Trials Regulation, 2014 and the preceding Clinical Trials Directive, 2001) to speed up clinical drug trials and streamline testing procedures across the European Union, all these regulatory changes led to a complete overhaul of the regulatory milieu in which CTs and new drugs are approved. See for instance, Hamowy (2010).
6. For a brief overview of the contradictory nature of the proposed amendments, see Barnes et al. (2015).

on 'bio-waivers'[7] for when to conduct bioequivalence studies, dictate the rate of their introduction in the Indian market (Gulhati 2003). Further, on the moral front, a threadbare ethics infrastructure together with a large pool of impoverished and benighted individuals allows scope for abuse where regulatory oversight is weak. The case for effectively regulating CTs becomes all the more important because these are studies done on human participants to determine the efficacy, safety or tolerance of new drugs, but may be conflated by a trial participant as the best available therapy, often referred to as 'therapeutic misconception'.[8]

This report limits discussion to the domain of CTs involving active interventions, focusing on 'NCEs' and 'New Drugs'.[9] The aim is to contextualise the debate around clinical research within the ambit of the new drug approval process in order to identify the challenges and prospects for clinical research in India from a regulatory standpoint. Likewise, we have developed actionable policy recommendations so that India can realise its untapped potential in the domain of clinical research, while addressing the concerns raised regarding the conduct and quality of CTs in the Indian context.

1.1 Regulating Clinical Research

Regulations are fundamental to the process of drug development and marketing. Policies and regulations are required to ensure that the end-product is safe for public use and responsive to their health needs. Further, the presence of multiple stakeholders in the pharmaceutical sector, including patients, health service providers, manufacturers and drug developers, requires regulations to guide each stakeholder in the sector. These regulations generally include provisions relating to manufacturing, distribution, import, marketing, labelling, prescribing and, sometimes, the pricing of pharmaceutical products.[10] This is done to ensure compliance with the best practices related to appropriate quality, safety and efficacy (the regulatory triad) of such products.

However, since CTs are experiments to establish the efficacy and safety of an entity on humans, there are potential concerns.[11] Hence, in addition to the aforementioned regulatory triad, the bioethical quad of autonomy, justice, beneficence and non-maleficence also comes into play in order to ensure ethical conduct of clinical research across the globe. The 'quad' safeguards, first and foremost, the rights of CT participants, their interests and safety. Although risks exist in such research, minimisation of the risks through cogent procedures and containment/mitigation of unanticipated risks are important aspects for the conduct of CTs.

Along with the changing burden of diseases, the requirement for developing newer and better drugs has also grown exponentially, which in turn, has led to growth in clinical investigations. In parallel, different regulations have been imposed and laws enacted to ensure that the discovered treatments and drugs are safe and effective for use. The sole purpose of such regulations for evaluation and approval of treatments is to minimise potential risks that such untested drugs might bear on human participants, especially of new drugs. Regulatory authorities around the world have adopted new principles, regulations and codes to respond better to public health needs. It has also been the case that regulations have evolved in the form of standards, and adherence to such standards has become the guiding light to ethicism and safety in clinical procedures and conduct. For instance, the Indian Good Clinical Practice (GCP) guidelines first appeared in 2001, and despite being guidelines, they are followed as regulatory standards. Similarly, the International Council on Harmonisation of Technical Requirements for Registration of Pharmaceuticals for Human Use (ICH) came up with a GCP framework (E6) and evaluation of the impact of ethnic factors

---

7. The term biowaiver is applied to a regulatory drug approval process where the efficacy and safety part of the dossier (application) is approved based on evidence of equivalence other than through in vivo equivalence testing. Based on biopharmceutics classification system (BCS), regulatory agencies like CDSCO, USFDA and even WHO can recommend for biowaivers to certain categories of drugs in order to ensure their easy accessibility. The term 'biowaiver' should not be conflated with a 'CT waiver'.

8. For instance, a research participant may conflate research with clinical care, sometimes underestimating risks and overestimating benefits, or both, in the hope for the best personal outcome. See, Horng and Grady (2003).

9. Trials pertaining to only drugs including small molecules; vaccines and biopharmaceuticals are discussed here. Those related to medical devices; surgeries; medical procedures and alternate systems of medicine including AYUSH etc, are out of the scope of this report and are hence not dealt here.

10. Chapter 6, Pharmaceutical Legislation and Regulation, Managing Access to Medicines and Health Technologies, WHO (2012).

11. These include concerns emanating from the innate toxicities of the composition, toxicities due to the interactions of the various drug components present in the formulation, and toxicities developed due to interaction with the human body.

(E5 (R1)) in 1996 and 1998 respectively for conducting CTs, and are referred to as standards in countries like the US, Japan, those in the EU and elsewhere. These standards of conduct also ensure that foreign clinical data in another country could be used for expediting drug approval process in a country, and as a consequence, pave the way for a more globalised clinical research landscape.

1.2 The Global Clinical Research Landscape

The global novel drug development front has had a tectonic shift in terms of how vertically integrated firms in the pharmaceutical industry—commonly referred to as Fully Integrated Pharmaceutical/Biopharmaceutical Company (FIPCO/FIBCO), operate. These entities increasingly rely on Contract Research Organisations (CROs) for undertaking global CT programmes. Concomitantly there is a qualitative shift from small molecule based drug discovery to an increasing number of biopharmaceuticals entering into the fray, with more drugs catering to an ever increasing burden of chronic diseases. Leading the charge have been firms in the United States (US)—the number of new medicines approved in the US has increased from 29 in 2006 to 51 in 2014, with more than 500 medicines being approved since 2000.[12] Further, across the globe there are more than 7,000 drug molecules undergoing development with over 70 per cent in various clinical phases[13] (see Figure 1.1). Globally, more than 210,000[14] CTs have been registered, with the US hosting over 43 per cent of them (see Table 1.1).

Over time, the average cost of developing a new drug has increased several times.[15] Since a large part of drug development costs is incurred in conducting CTs, pharmaceutical companies have reportedly moved to newer destinations in order to conduct these trials economically, among several other factors, without compromising on the quality of trials.[16] Some other key factors cited in the literature for the shift of trial sites to less developed countries include emerging markets due to higher growth in them, availability of skilled professionals, larger treatment-naïve populations,[17] with higher patient recruitment rates and retention. Hence, pharmaceutical firms are increasingly shifting CTs to East, South and Southeast Asia (see Figure 1.2).

Table 1.1
Contribution of Select Countries to Clinical Research (CTs Registered)

Country	Population (millions)	Clinical Trials	Trials per million
Canada	36	14,846	413
United States	322	90,550	281
United Kingdom	65	11,470	177
South Korea	50	6,891	137
South Africa	55	2,130	39
Japan	127	3,958	31
Brazil	208	4,815	23
Mexico	127	2,519	20
India	1,311	2,768	2

Source: World Population 2015 (Population Division, United Nations); Clinical trials.gov (accessed on March 16, 2016).

As the number of CTs has increased, the demand for larger pools of human patients has also gone up. Over the years, patient recruitment and retention for CTs has become more difficult. The global patient enrolment rates dropped from 75 per cent in 2000 to 59 per cent in 2006, along with a 21 per cent drop in retention rates over the same time period.[18] The costs of enrolling patients for CTs have increased like all other costs and the inefficiency in retaining patients has led to the shift in trial sites to regions with larger population pools. To add to this, the relatively affluent

---

12. *Pharmaceutical Industry Profile* 2007 and 2015, Pharmaceutical Research and Manufacturers of America.
13. Ibid.
14. As per the number of registrations on *clinicaltrials.gov* as on 16 March 2016. Although this is not a globally representative/inclusive registry, but is one of the largest and most comprehensive. See Appendix III for a more detailed description of CT registries and their evolution.
15. The multifold rise in cost of drug development is worked out by including 'sunk costs' incurred while undertaking failed global drug development programmes, as well as 'time costs' incurred to undertake these clinical programmes. These costs represent almost two thirds of the total drug development costs. The 3rd Pharmaceutical Congress Asia, 2016 held at Singapore, opened with a corporate presentation where the current cost of novel drug discovery was quoted to be in excess of US$ 3 billion. This figure is higher than the currently contested estimate by almost US $ 0.5 billion.
16. According to Garnier (2008), a first-rate academic medical centre in India charges $1,500-$2,000 per patient case report, while a second-rate centre in the US charged ten times that amount. In addition, clinical costs include human and physical capital expenses which are also available at a lesser cost in developing countries, generating significant savings for companies.
17. Treatment-naïve patients are those who have never taken medications similar to the new drug before. It is easier to study the efficacy of a new drug in such patients.
18. The Numbers Game: Boosting Clinical Trial Enrolment (2014), *www.pharmaceutical-technology.com* (Last accessed on 11 February 2017).

Figure 1.1

Clinical Trials Phases: A Quick Primer

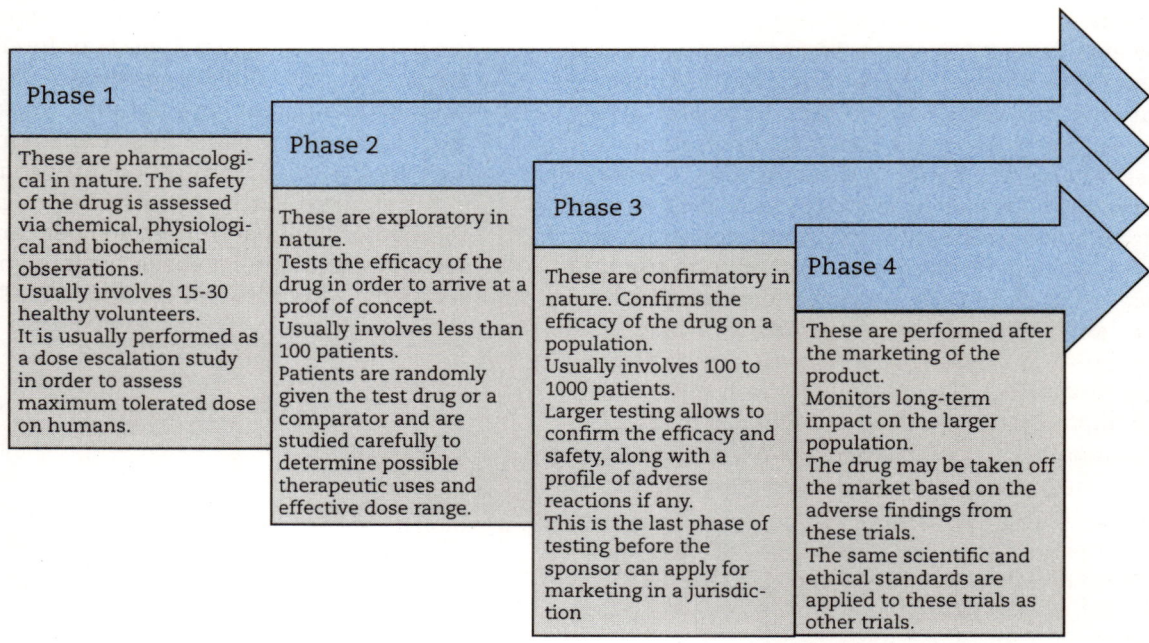

Phase 1
- These are pharmacological in nature. The safety of the drug is assessed via chemical, physiological and biochemical observations.
- Usually involves 15-30 healthy volunteers.
- It is usually performed as a dose escalation study in order to assess maximum tolerated dose on humans.

Phase 2
- These are exploratory in nature.
- Tests the efficacy of the drug in order to arrive at a proof of concept.
- Usually involves less than 100 patients.
- Patients are randomly given the test drug or a comparator and are studied carefully to determine possible therapeutic uses and effective dose range.

Phase 3
- These are confirmatory in nature. Confirms the efficacy of the drug on a population.
- Usually involves 100 to 1000 patients.
- Larger testing allows to confirm the efficacy and safety, along with a profile of adverse reactions if any.
- This is the last phase of testing before the sponsor can apply for marketing in a jurisdiction

Phase 4
- These are performed after the marketing of the product.
- Monitors long-term impact on the larger population.
- The drug may be taken off the market based on the adverse findings from these trials.
- The same scientific and ethical standards are applied to these trials as other trials.

Figure 1.2

Relative Number versus Percentual Substitution Per Region in 2006 and 2012

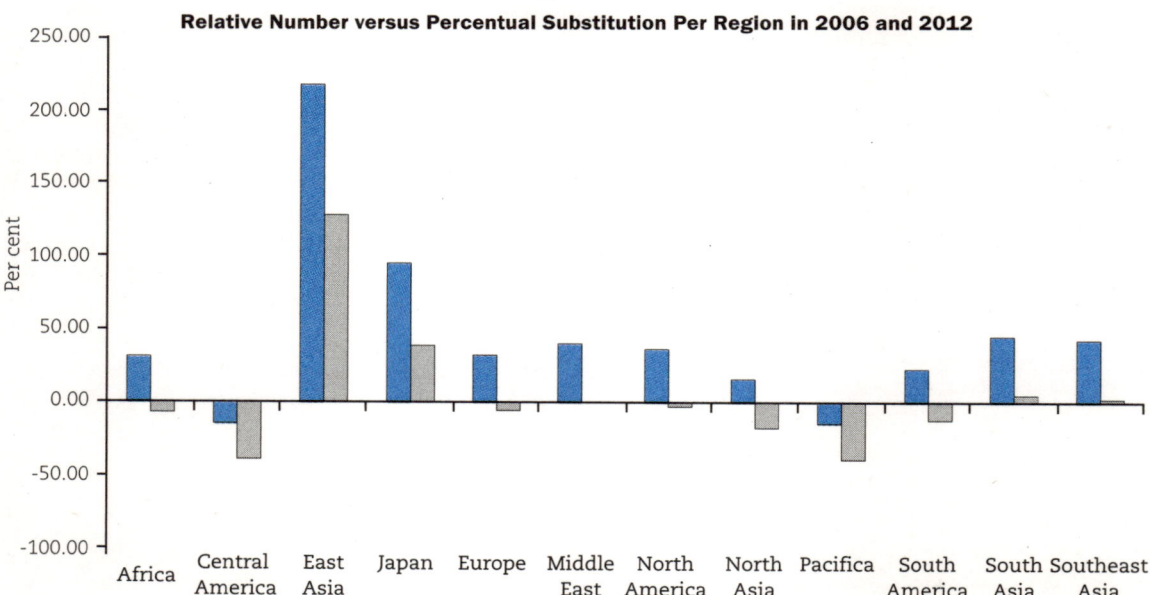

Notes: Blue Bar denotes growth in the no. of CTs registered in the region between 2006 and 2012; Grey Bar denotes growth in the percentage share of each region in global CTs between 2006 and 2012.

Source: Novak et al. (2014).*

---

* Available at, http://www.appliedclinicaltrialsonline.com/decline-clinical-trials-central-and-eastern-europe-fluctuation-or-trend. Last accessed on 4 April 2017.

populations in developed countries are becoming 'treatment saturated',[19] which reduces the capacity to prove the effectiveness of new drugs, making the results less statistically valid (Petryna 2005).

The increase in CTs around the globe and the shift towards developing countries has clear benefits like faster development of new drugs, quicker access to patients, knowledge and expertise transfer to the developing regions and access to medications, which was otherwise difficult in these regions.[20] Moreover some trials are meant to study medical conditions that may be endemic to developing countries, which can only be performed with participation from the local population pool. However, it is construed that the ease of accessibility to regions with inadequate regulatory framework and largely uninformed populations has its own set of challenges for conducting clinical research, and shall be broadly discussed in a later section with relevant data.

1.3 The Indian Clinical Research Growth Story

With globalisation of CTs, India emerged as one of the highly attractive trial sites in the world. Over time, India's share in the global CTs market increased from 0.9 per cent in 2008 to 5 per cent in 2013 (Mondal and Abrol 2015). This initial shift of trial sites to India was taken to be the result of all the aforementioned factors. According to AT Kearney's Country Attractiveness Index, India was the second most attractive site (after China) for conducting CTs outside the US.[21] Further, according to Cambridge Healthtech Associates' survey of 235 pharmaceutical executives in 2006, over three-fourths of the top 50 Western biopharmaceutical companies were conducting drug development activities in India, more than in any other emerging country.[22]

As part of the trade liberalisation agenda, India became a signatory to the General Agreement on Tariffs and Trade (GATT) in 1994, and in 1995, signed the WTO Trade-Related Aspects of Intellectual Property Rights (TRIPS)[23] agreement. In 2005, India amended its patent laws to fully comply with the agreement. At the same time, India removed phase-lag[24] for CTs to allow multi-country concurrent trials in the country. Further, to attract foreign pharma companies, India permitted 100 per cent FDI in this sector, thus making it easier for foreign companies to set up base in India and conduct CTs. This added to India showcasing itself as a favourable destination for conducting CTs and witnessed a concomitant rise in the number of CTs (see Figure 1.3).

However, today, public opinion in India is not quite in favour of CTs as several CROs have been blamed for conducting trials without due concern for procedural and ethical issues. This culminated into a petition being filed at the Supreme Court of India against inadequate regulations for conducting global CTs in India (see Appendix V for a brief timeline of events that impacted clinical research in India). This led to a flurry of interim orders and directions to the government, following which the sudden rise witnessed in the conduct of CTs in India came to a halt.[25] In July 2013, the US National Institutes of Health (NIH) reportedly suspended 40 CTs in India because of uncertainties created by and strictness of the new requirements. While the petition is still pending before the Supreme

---

19. Treatment saturated patients are those who are already using medicines for various illness/diseases and therefore, enrolling them as patients for the study of a new drug becomes difficult as the efficacy of the new drug cannot be studied in isolation because of the existing medicines being used by the patient.
20. In several instances, patients participating in trials in developing regions benefit from the access to some yet to be registered medicines, which elsewhere may have become either the next line of therapy or the routine standard of care.
21. See, https://www.atkearney.com/documents/10192/312631/EA+vol+IX+no+1Make+Your+Move.pdf/bb05c14b-2709-4ff1-828f-8ef851f303de (Last accessed on 4 April 2017).
22. *Globalization of Drug Development: India* (2006). Cambridge Healthtech Associates.
23. TRIPS is a multilateral agreement administered by World Trade Organization (WTO) to set up the standards for protection of intellectual property rights and are applied uniformly to all WTO member states. The agreement has three basic features, standards, enforcement and dispute settlements related to IP rights.
24. A phase lag meant that phase II trial could be conducted in India only after phase III trials were completed elsewhere. Schedule Y of the D&C Rules was amended in 2005 to remove this lag and allow concurrent global CTs.
25. As already mentioned, DCG(I) approved only 19 CTs in 2013, a drop of roughly 93 per cent from 2012 (262 trials), and represents a fraction of its peak of 500 trials in 2010.

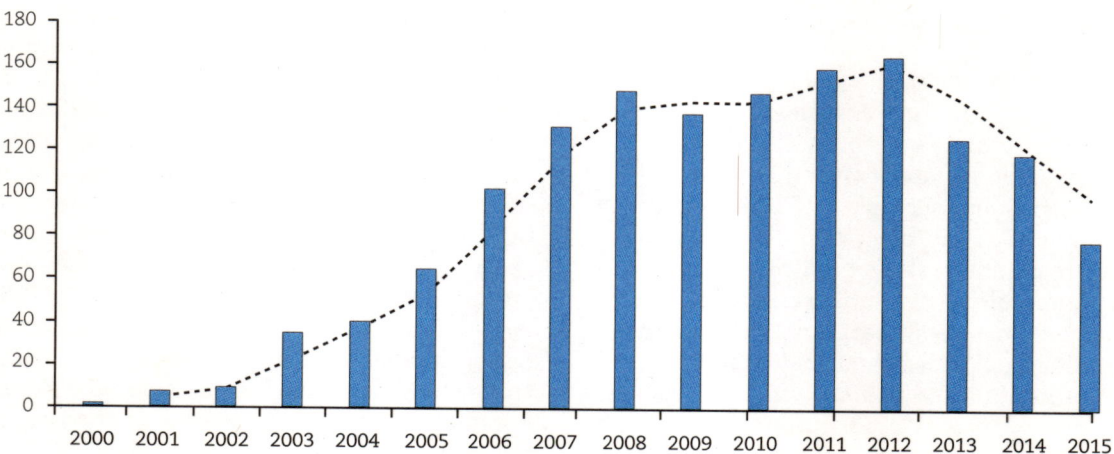

Figure 1.3
Growth of Global Clinical Trials in India: 2000 and 2015

Source: Clinicaltrials.gov (accessed on 2 February 2016).

Court, there have been frequent regulatory changes during this period (see Annexure VI).[26]

Against this background, this report attempts to situate the locus and focus of the practice of clinical research in India. It is divided into four sections. The next section describes the research methodology. Section 3 deals with significance and dilemmas associated with clinical research at large and in developing countries like India in particular. Regulations in various countries under study are also discussed. Section 4 briefly discusses the Indian clinical research scenario and some of the critical issues that have cropped up, comparing its regulations with that in other countries. And finally we have a concluding section.

---

26. The growing pressure and the recent orders by the Supreme Court in the Swasthya Adhikar Manch paved way for the Government of India proposing amendments to the current Drugs and Cosmetics Act, 1940 by tabling a new bill. The draft of the Drugs and Cosmetics (Amendment) Bill, 2015 came into the public domain on 31st December, 2014 and public comments were invited till the 12th of January, 2015. This draft has now been withdrawn and instead a complete overhaul in the D&C Act is envisioned.

2

Research Methodology

The study employs a mixed methodology with both desk and field research. The latter was conducted nationally across selected zones/industrial clusters in India and in some international jurisdictions based on semi-structured interviews. For the national round of field work, apart from stakeholders in Delhi (CDSCO, MoHFW, civil society bodies, industry groups, corporate representatives), the interviews were conducted in clusters where clinical research activity is found to be maximum or major pharmaceutical firms are located (Maharashtra, Gujarat, Andhra Pradesh, Bangalore etc.), whereas for the purpose of international benchmarking, all the jurisdictions which contribute most to the new drug development (see Table 2.1) are suited for this study. The 'sample set' of international jurisdictions represent those from the ICH region as well as those outside it, and represent both developed and developing nations. International benchmarking was used to chart out challenges the clinical industry faces and derive policy lessons for clinical research and the new drug approval process in India.

primarily based on the number of registered CTs. Out of them, amongst the top countries in the former— USA and UK—and amongst the latter: South Africa was chosen.[1] Singapore, Germany and Indonesia were chosen as part of convenience sampling. Table 2.1 highlights that the pharmaceutical industry in the selected countries—South Africa and Indonesia – is predominantly generic, akin to the Indian context, while US, Singapore and UK are a mix of both— something which Indian policymakers and industry should probably aspire to, and hence closely look at. Countries/Regions from both the former and latter category were finally selected for field research, based on the analysis of key regulatory provisions from where policy lessons for India can be drawn.

As the policy and regulations, affecting CTs constitute a major part of the new drug development process, various stakeholders were interviewed for the study (See Table 2.2). The interviewees belonged to a broad spectrum of experts, including government regulators, retired government officials/policymakers,

Table 2.1

Country/Region Selection Criteria

Country	CT Density (per million population)	Number of Registered CTs*	Predominant Pharmaceutical Industry Type	Deaths Due to NCDs	WB Income Classification
India	2.12	2785	Generic	High	Non-High
Israel	665.5	5367	NCE/ Generic	Low	High
United States	272.9	87804	NCE /Generic	High	High
Canada	399.3	14349	NCE /Generic	Mid	High
United Kingdom	170.0	11007	NCE/Generic	High	High
Singapore	267.4	1499	NCE/Generic	Low	High
Brazil	22.3	4642	Generic	High	Non-high
Mexico	19.2	2437	Generic	High	Non-high
South Africa	38.3	2089	Generic	Mid	Non-high
Thailand	26.2	1778	Generic	High	Non-high

Note: * clinicaltrial.gov.

2.1 Country Selection Criteria

We used a multi-dimensional approach to shortlist countries/regions from both the developed and developing parts of the world. To begin with, we calculated CT densities (2015) and shortlisted top 20 countries which were in the high income category and top 20 in the non-high income category. As the next step, we selected six countries in both categories

academicians, physicians (investigators of CTs), industry representatives (sponsors of CTs), FDA consultants, CROs, bioethicists etc. A portfolio of the potential stakeholders in India and abroad was populated with the help of an advisory panel in order to better understand the ground situation.

---

1. Brazil, Mexico and Thailand were experiencing the Zika epidemic, the next country in the list i.e. South Africa was chosen.

Table 2.2

Cross-section of Respondents across Disciplines and Occupations

Representative Category of Interviewees	Number of Interviewees	
	National	International
Drug regulators/policymakers	2	26
Ethics committee members	4	5
Academicians/practitioners	50	25
Legal experts	4	12
Civil society members	2	4
Industry representatives	18	19
Contract Research Organisations*	13	6
Industry associations	5	9
Independent consultants	4	1
Multilateral institutions	0	7
Total	92	114

Note: *Includes clinical trial units, SMOs, providing support to all aspects of clinical research.

The qualitative data collected from the ground was backed by quantitative data from resources like ClinicalTrials.gov and Clinical Trial Registry of India (CTRI), existing scientific literature and databases like PubMed, etc. (For a detailed note on CT registries, refer to Appendix IV). But primarily records from CTRI were analysed in order to get a representative trend of the Indian clinical research milieu. (See Figure 2.1). All entries from the CTRI database were exported to Strata 3.1 and further populated and individually analysed for relevant data points.

Figure 2.1

Algorithm* Followed for Screening Records in CTRI Database

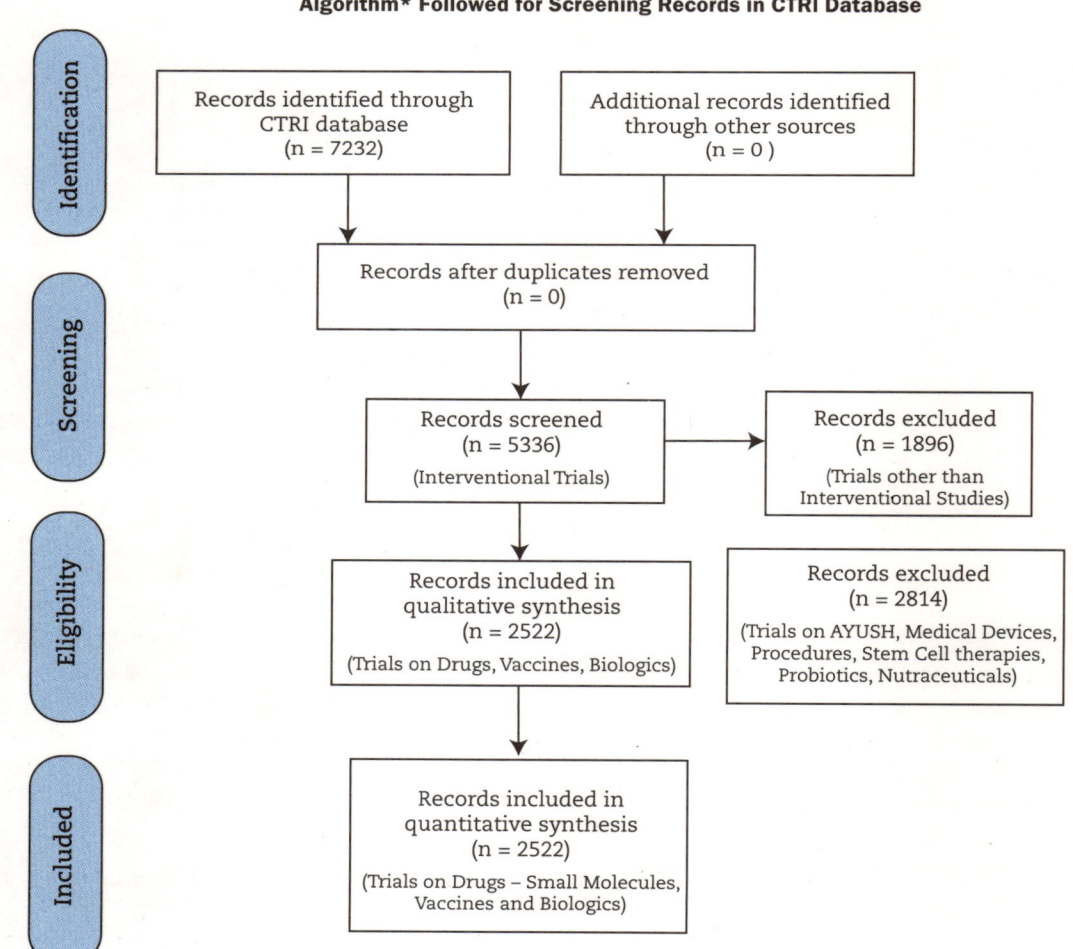

Note: * Adapted from PRISMA (2009) methodology. CTRI records identified as on 2 September 2016.

3

The Dilemmas Afflicting Clinical Research in India

3.1 Overview

Clinical research is the endeavour to advance knowledge while practicing clinical medicine whereas CTs are a key research tool to advance this body of medical knowledge and bring safe and efficacious therapies for patients. A CT may be a part of a clinical development programme for a novel drug with the intent of applying for a marketing authorisation or to evaluate the safety or efficacy of medicines already in practice for new indications/ route of administration; compare different doses/ therapeutic regimens. Both commercial entities as well as members of the academic community can undertake CTs with either a commercial mandate or for publication and/or development or revision of existing therapeutic guidelines (Griffin 2009).

Although the objectives ascribed to CTs are noble, they are often afflicted by several oxymoronic forks. To make things worse, there is lack of adequate data in the public domain on clinical research: a) firms may withhold clinical data as part of a larger corporate strategy; b) regulations/compulsions of intellectual property may prohibit a regulatory body from disclosing information; c) the absence of adequate data capturing mechanisms can have similar outcomes. Hence, the body of knowledge relating to clinical research in several regulatory jurisdictions tends to be restricted and sometimes be rather tacit. Absence of adequate data and regulatory guidance on key issues in such a scenario can lead to ever convoluted misperceptions. The current debate on the conduct of clinical research in India is afflicted with several such inconsistencies. From the secondary literature and interviews conducted, we identified three paradoxical inconsistencies which seem to have evolved with the current debate:

3.1.1 Need for Evidence based Medicine: To go Global or Local?

Measuring health and economic impacts of research is generally problematic. Critically done 'systematic reviews' and studies based on 'meta-analysis' of clinical research data are recognised as one of the best source for generating evidence on safety and efficacy of a healthcare intervention.[1] Policy interventions are contingent on the worth of this underlying medical evidence, hence the need for 'evidence based medicine' necessarily mandates that population relevant trials are instituted. This entails that a statistically significant number of participants from the local population participate in a CT, where the clinical end points for safety and efficacy are adequately met and analysed.

As previously mentioned, CTs for NCEs are often done as part of a concurrent global drug development programme which translates to multi-country, multi-site global CTs[2] involving hundreds if not thousands of participants in later stages of development (phase 3 and 4). However, for introduction of new drugs by Indian firms in India, CTs often tend to be lagged behind phase 3 trials or bridging studies involving 100-200 patients. (See Table 3.1).

In India, out of 7,232 registered clinical studies,[3] 74 per cent or 5,336 studies are classified as interventional trials (see Figure 3.1) and are germane to the debate on CTs in India. Out of these interventional studies, only 2,522 or 48 per cent studies involve administration of allopathic entities drugs/small molecules (2065, 39%); biologics (256, 5%) and vaccines (201, 4%). The other 52 per cent studies[4] involves interventions either based on alternate systems of medicine (AYUSH), probiotics or surgical procedures/use of medical devices etc. (constituting the category of non-drugs) (see Figure 3.2).

Out of the 2,522 studies, 902 studies or 37 per cent are sponsored by national and international non-profit agencies combined. Not very far behind are the trials sponsored by foreign/global firms still which stands at 864 studies and constitute 34 per cent of the total, while the Indian pharmaceutical firms have sponsored 728 studies constituting 29 per cent of the total interventional trials under study (See Figure 3.3).

Over 81 per cent of the trials sponsored by foreign firms are multicounty trials, while 97 per cent of the trials sponsored by both Indian firms as well as non-profit agencies (Indian and foreign combined) respectively are locally instituted trials (see Figure 3.4).

---

1. See for instance, The Cochrane Database for Systematic Reviews.
2. However it should be duly noted that not all GCTs are for NCEs. A GCT may be done to explore or confirm new clinical indications/new dosage forms/new route of administration for an already approved drug.
3. CTRI data analysed here is from the beginning of the year 2007 to 2nd September 2016. The year of conduct of a trial and the year of its registration need not be the same, because until 15th June 2009, it was not mandatory to register a trial with CTRI. Hence, several studies have been registered retrospectively and likewise prospectively.
4. The analysis is restricted to only the former category of interventions involving small molecules, biologics and vaccines. The latter category of interventions although are relevant to clinical research, lie out of the scope of the discussion presented here.

Figure 3.1

Registered Clinical Trial in India: Trial Type Profile

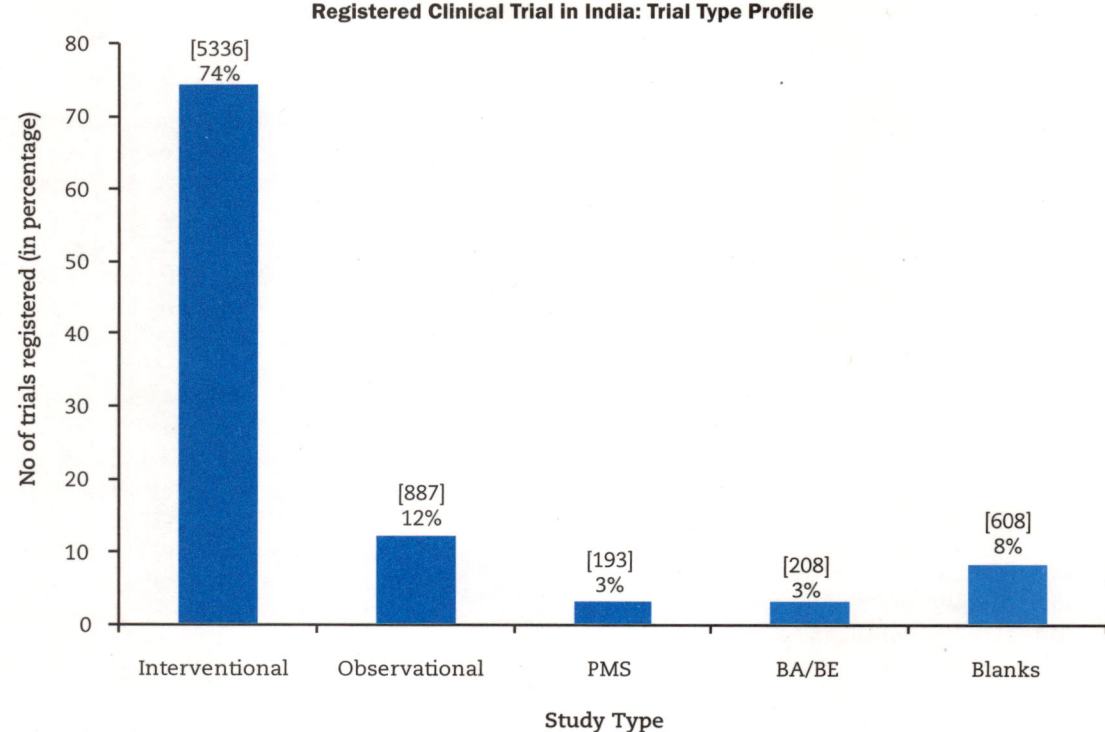

Notes: Interventional: Active intervention on trial participation; Observational: No active intervention, e.g.: Epidemiological survey; PMS: Post Marketing Surveillance to generate long term safety profile (not to be confused with Phase 4 Trials); BA/BE: Bioavailability/Bioequivalence studies, for introducing generics or filing ANDA applications abroad; Blanks: Study type not assigned.

Source: Own compilation from CTRI.

Figure 3.2

Registered Clinical Trials in India: Intervention Type Profile

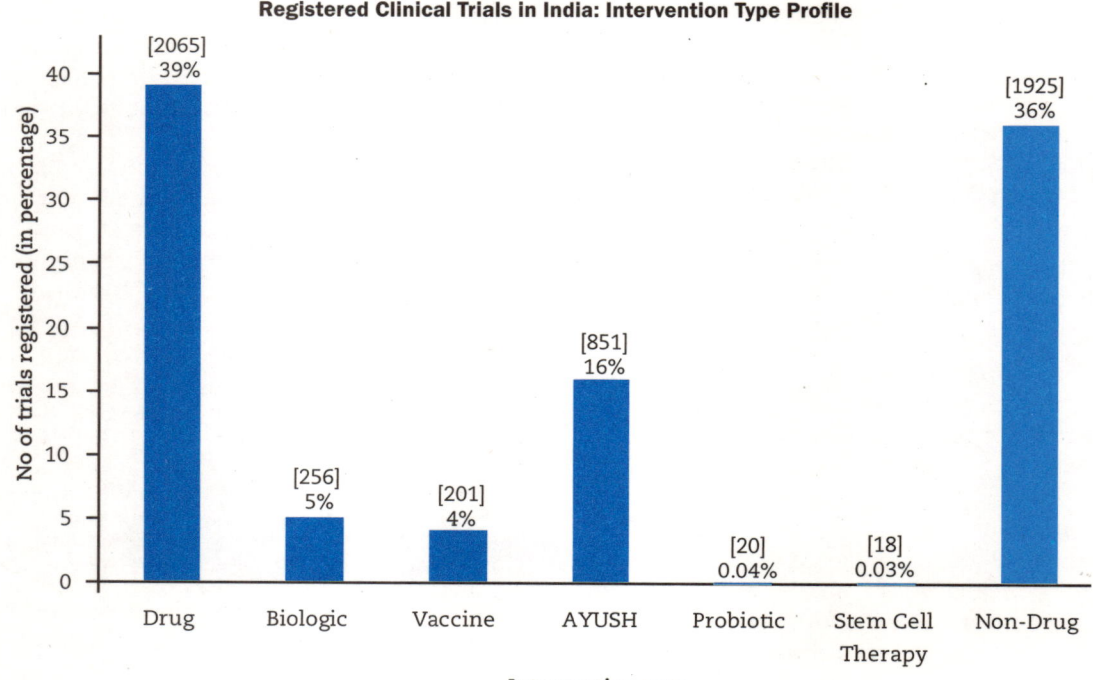

Notes: Break up of interventional trials registered in CTRI.

Source: Own compilation from CTRI.

Figure 3.3

Registered Clinical Trials in India: Sponsor Profile

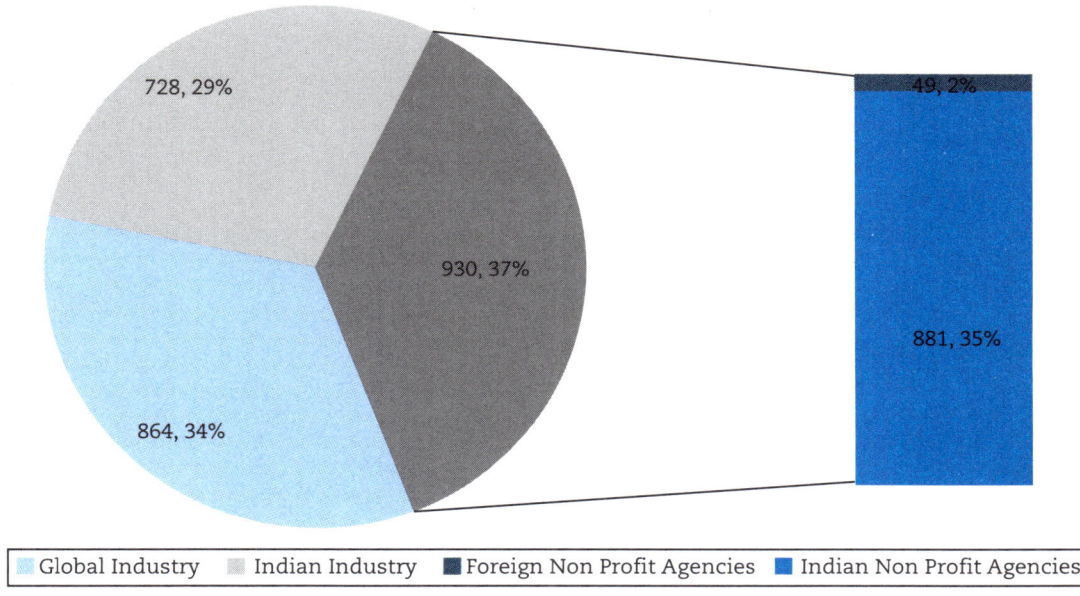

Global Industry | Indian Industry | Foreign Non Profit Agencies | Indian Non Profit Agencies

Source: Own compilation from CTRI.

Table 3.1

Comparison of Phase 3 Global Clinical Trials vs Local Clinical Trials

Trial Characteristic	Global Clinical Trial	Local Clinical Trial
Primarily sponsored by	Foreign firms	Indian firms
Multi-country	More than 88 per cent trials	Less than 3 per cent trials
Multi-site	Majority done over 8 sites	Majority done under 5 sites
Subjects involved	Majority done with over 500+ participants	Majority done with less than 200 participants
CT application approved	~86 per cent* (1 Jan–30 June 2012)	~99 per cent^

Source: Own compilation from CTRI; * Casefiles: W.P. No. 33/2012; ^ Personal Communication (Office of DCG(I)).

Over 66 per cent of these trials are comprised of either phase 3 or 4. Out of the studies labelled as only phase 3 studies (1092), over 53 per cent are sponsored by foreign firms, mostly representative of GCTs, while 35 per cent of these are sponsored by Indian firms, mostly representative of bridging studies, the remaining 12 per cent phase 3 trials are sponsored by non-profit agencies (see Figure 3.5 and Table 3.1).

Several leading pharmacologists and clinical investigators (national and international) interviewed concurred that a GCT programme aiming to include as many participants from racially and ethnically diverse groups would render far more robust results in contrast to bridging studies. By pooling data from several countries and ensuring that the statistical analysis is not underpowered, a far better evidence can be generated.

In contrast, the local CTs are either warranted for diseases endemic to the local country which mandates participation from the local population pool or are mostly phase 3 bridging studies so as to weed out those drugs that can show markedly different clinical/pharmacological behaviour in

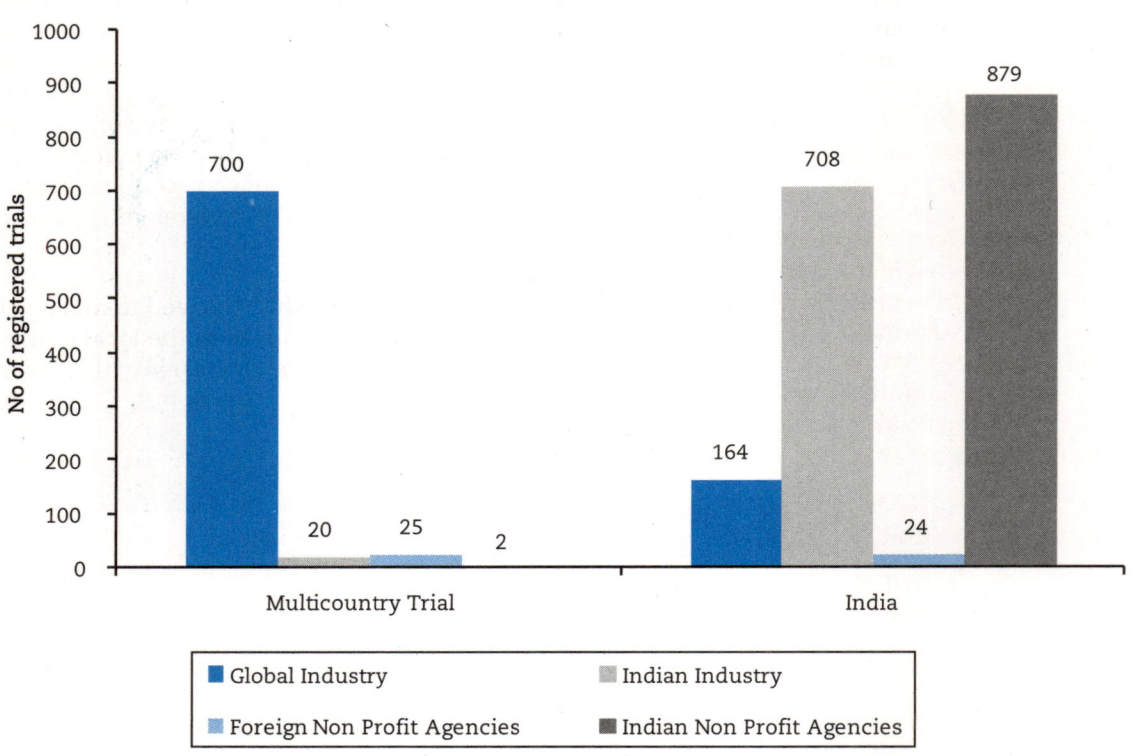

Figure 3.4

Registered Clinical Trials: Sponsor-site Profile

Source: Own compilation from CTRI.

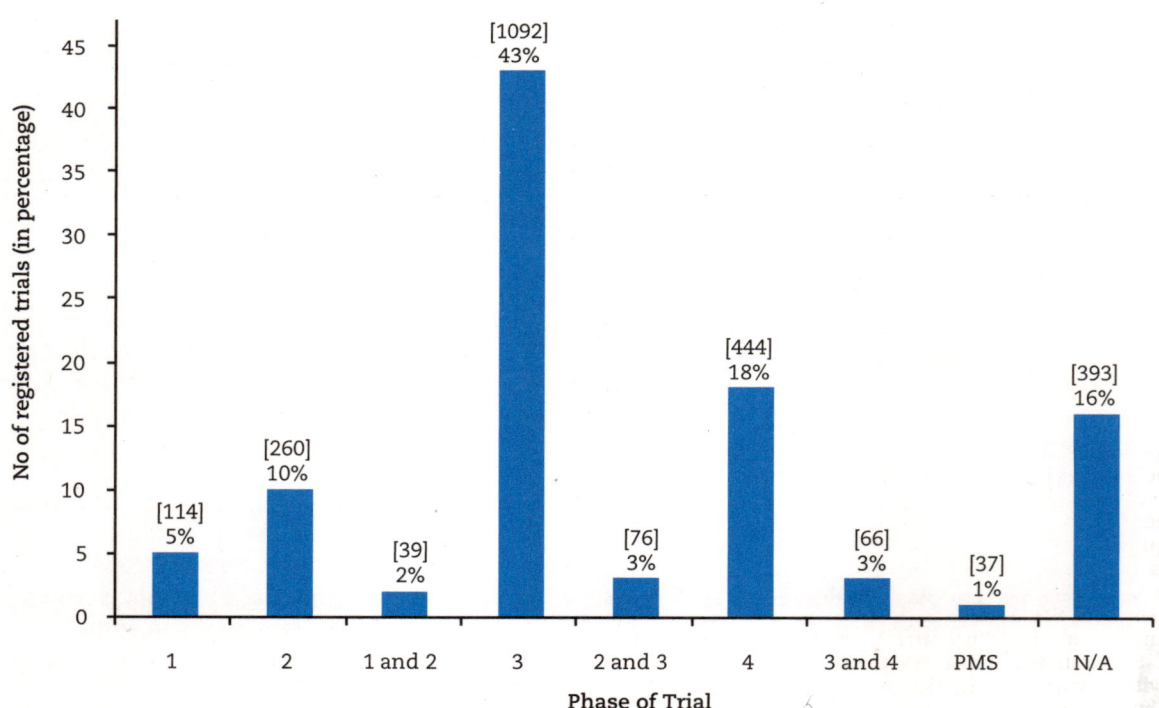

Figure 3.5

Registered Clinical Trials in India: Phase Profile

Source: Own compilation from CTRI.

different ethnicities.[5] Trials for endemic diseases is an absolute necessity however for the latter, although the oft cited reason is to establish safety, majority of the stakeholders interviewed conveyed that they are of little scientific value as they largely serve the purpose of crossing a regulatory hurdle.[6] This can be summarised from the following statement from a key opinion leader:

> In case of India how does one define who is Indian? The diversity inside India between different ethnic groups is perhaps bigger than difference with non-Indians! The big question is HOW TO DEFINE who is a local person in India. If the definition is not given, the requirement (of instituting a local clinical trial) is scientifically nonsense.
>
> —Key Opinion Leader, International Multilateral Institution

Hence a demand is often raised that in order to ensure faster availability of relevant drugs to the masses, CTs for certain therapeutic categories and given conditions should be altogether waived.[7] Noted experts that were interviewed conveyed that although instating a mechanism where the Indian regulator can rely on the regulatory evaluation of strict drug regulatory authorities is a good idea, but it may not be implemented, given the prevailing adverse sentiments around the sector.

The 'adverse sentiments' mentioned echoes the protest against the waivers granted for CTs and the charge that untested drugs are allowed to enter the Indian market without evidence of safety or efficacy. So in essence, on the one hand for the want of evidence, local clinical trials in developing countries like India are demanded, while concomitantly the charge is made that pharmaceutical firms increasingly offshore CTs to developing countries via GCTs.

The conundrum lies with the need to make new and relevant drugs available in the local market and the conflict with the uncertainty that equipoise entails, which necessitates elaborate CTs in order to generate adequate scientific evidence. This oxymoron is demonstrated with the perceptions different quarters hold for concurrent vis-á-vis lagged drug development.

3.1.2 Notions About Risk Involved in a Clinical Trial and Risk Across a Clinical Trial Programme

To be able to comprehend the involved oxymoron, it is important to define 'risk' involved in a CT. The primary aim of conducting a CT is disparaged by many, citing the 'safety compromise' of the participants. The opponents to CTs quote ethical principles and label CTs as unfair for exposing trial participants to the risks of an experiment for potential benefits to others. Here, clinical equipoise becomes very important for carrying out a trial. According to the principle of equipoise,[8] a particular patient may be enrolled in a CT only as long as the physician or community of physicians remain uncertain about relative therapeutic merits of interventions to which participants could be randomly assigned in a trial.

The oxymoron emerges with the varying perception over the degree of risk involved along a clinical development programme and trials in general. To illustrate, for first-in-human studies such as Phase 1 studies (although in most cases there is no clinical benefit to the individual),[9] there is always some degree of risk involved, but this is minimised by the small amounts of drug that is administered and the careful monitoring of the volunteer for any

---

5. However, an anomaly in this argument can be noted that several CROs in India, have not been marketing 'India' as a hotspot of ethnic diversity rather an extension of the larger Central Asian Caucasian belt.
6. Data from CTRI shows that most phase 3 clinical trials conducted by Indian Industry are bridging trials. In India apart from one instance, till date, no marketing application with data from a bridging trial has ever led to a rejection on account of deviant results from the global clinical data. (Personal Communication from the office of DCG(I)).
7. Rule 122A in DCR, 1945, states, "Provided that the requirement of submitting the results of local clinical trials may not be necessary if the drug is of such a nature that the Licensing Authority may, in public interest decide to grant such permission on the basis of data available from other countries.", and hence provides for the waiver of the requirement of local clinical trials in India. An idea was mooted during the regime of the erstwhile DCG(I) that for applications with clinical data evaluated by certain predefined regulatory jurisdictions classified as 'strict', the requirement of local clinical trial may be waived off, but this was never brought into practice. However a similar provision was brought via an office order in 2015 for biosimilars. See Appendix VI, entry 16a. This idea is again doing rounds in policy circles, see for instance, Agenda No. S-2, minutes of the 75th meeting of Drugs Technical Advisory Board (DTAB), held on 3rd January, 2017. Available at: http://www.cdsco.nic.in/writereaddata/Minutes%20of%2075th%20DTAB%20held%20on%2003_01_2017.pdf (Last accessed on 4 April 2017).
8. Fried (1974) referred to this as a state of uncertainty—being equally poised between available options.
9. Although this is true for the most part, however for certain terminal illnesses (for instance Stage IV Cancer), a Phase 1 may also act as an exploratory trial if the volunteer/participant is a patient, who can be rendered with a net therapeutic gain.

adverse signs caused by the drug.[10] The risk to the population increases as a trial advances, with more participants are given greater cumulative amounts of the drug under less controlled conditions (Muller and Husar 2013). However, with every additional subject participating, the clinical experience with the drug grows, thereby decreasing the associated clinical equipoise by providing a greater safety profile in humans. In other words, later in the programme, when treating patients with a disease, there is a possible, but unproven, benefit that they may be cured or symptoms may be alleviated. The risk to the individual therefore should intuitively decrease as the clinical programme progresses. However, it is also argued that as the numbers of participants in early stages of clinical trials is low and data from the toxicology studies is fairly limited, more exposure in later stages of CTs may reveal evidence of a hitherto undetected form of toxicity.

This conundrum along with the lack of clarity with data and the source of data[11] on the occurrence of total number of Serious Adverse Events (SAEs) during CTs in India, further complicates the issue. In a ministry note, it was initially said that a total 1,514 participants had died between 2008 to August, 2010 during CTs. This was updated and it was said that between 1 January 2005 to 30 June 2012; 57,303 participants took part in CTs and 39,022 of them completed the CTs. A total of 11,972 SAEs (see Table 3.3) occurred during this period and 2,644 deaths occurred during these CTs,[12] out of which 80 (about 3 per cent) were related to CTs. In 44 cases of deaths, compensation was paid while there was no data for compensation records previous to 2008. It was further stated that between, 1 January 2005 till 2012 end; 2,868 deaths occurred during CTs, but only 89 (about 3 per cent) out of these were related to clinical trials. It was further stated that from January 2005 to December 2013, a total of 14,320 SAEs had occurred during CTs and 3,458 deaths occurred during this period.

According to data collated from several communications from various stakeholders, from January 2005 to September 2016; a total of 19,583 SAEs leading to an injury occurred during CTs (see Table 3.3), while 4,534 deaths occurred during CTs and compensation has been paid in over 160 cases, while the same was under examination for the year 2016 (see Table 3.2).

Table 3.2

SAEs (Death) Reported During the Period of 2005 to 2016

S.No.	Year	No. of SAEs Leading to Death During a CT	No. of Deaths Related to Clinical Trial	No. of Compensation Paid Cases
1	2005	128	5	5
2	2006	137	2	2
3	2007	136	4	4
4	2008	288	8	8
5	2009	637	16	16
6	2010	668	22	22
7	2011	438	16	16
8	2012	436	16	17
9	2013	590	NA	45
10	2014	443	NA	21
11	2015	381	NA	4
12	2016*	252	NA	Under examination
Total		4,534	160+	

Legends: * Till 30 September 2016.
Source: Personal Communication from a party to writ petition no. 33 of 2012.

It is important that a distinction is made between deaths/injuries occurring during a CT and deaths/injuries related to a CT. Globally, a sponsor is liable to pay compensation only in the cases where an analysis for 'relatedness'[13] attributes an SAE with the investigational product.

---

10. It was reiterated on several occasions that except for the exceptional and rare instance of the TeGenero first in human trial in UK that led to debilitating outcomes for the volunteers, the conduct of Phase 1 studies have been quite satisfactory. It was added that most Phase 3 trials are conducted in out-patient settings, while all Phase 1 trials are conducted in in-patient settings under highly controlled conditions, rendering more protection for the participant.
11. During field interviews it was found to be often conjectured that the data provided by the Ministry of Health, was collated by sponsors of clinical trials and there were no in-house records maintained. It is further conjectured that clinical investigators are on the pay rolls of the sponsor and hence have an interest in under reporting the figures on SAEs. However, in all the countries visited the ultimate source of SAE reporting during clinical trials or even otherwise was the clinical investigator (directly in touch with the participant or his/her kin) which has to report an SAE (death/injury) to both the Sponsors of the CT; the Ethics Committees as well as the National Drug Regulatory Authority.
12. The latter figure on SAEs leading to death is mutually exclusive to the former figure of total SAEs leading to injuries.
13. In an analysis for relatedness, a chosen 'causality' scale is reduced to the binary scale of 'relatedness' where an SAE (death or injury) is either related or not related to the investigational product. For more details refer to Section 4.

Table 3.3

SAEs (Injury) Reported During the Period of 2005 to 2016

S.No.	Year	No. of SAEs leading to injury during a CT (not caused due to or related to)	No. of Related SAEs	No. of Compensation Paid Cases
1	2005		1	NA
2	2006		22	NA
3	2007		14	NA
4	2008		46	NA
5	2009	11, 972	86	NA
6	2010		85	NA
7	2011		140	NA
8	2012	1226	112	NA
	Jan-June		NA	NA
	July-Dec			
9	2013	1, 122	NA	145
10	2014	1, 326	NA	94
11	2015	2, 359	NA	55
12	2016*	1, 578	NA	Under examination
Total		19, 583		

Legends: * Till 30 September 2016.
Source: Personal Communication from a party to Writ Petition no. 33 of 2012.

This unpredictability with risk 'in' and 'across' a clinical trial programme can play havoc with public policy stances in developing countries, which becomes all the more acute because CTs increasingly occur on a global scale as industry and sponsors in developed countries move trials to developing countries.[14] Efficient communication between the trial participants and investigators is important for reducing the severity of any potential risk and implementation of risk-minimising procedures. However, in developing countries, maintaining contact with the participants is difficult. The quality and effectiveness of the ethical procedures in a country depends upon its social institutions and political actions. The less influence of the civil society, higher is the incidence of risk with clinical research. Social monitoring of the research activities has major implications for risk-minimisation. Sometimes, the studies are carried out without the proper knowledge of the individual and/or the society at large. Besides, in case of adverse events, the dissemination of information to the society and the scientific community is made more difficult.

From a health policy perspective, the question remains whether a regulatory jurisdiction in such a condition, should allow the early participation of its citizens in a global clinical development programme or wait until the sponsor applies for a marketing authorisation and ask for a bridging trial. India is an example where the latter approach has been adopted for the most part of the history of clinical research for novel drug discovery. The end result being, most trials in India are phase 3 trials to confirm efficacy of the drug on Indian population (see Figure 3.5). But as the situation began to change, the regulatory overhaul in 2013 stymied the shift towards the global approach, further fuelling the oxymoronic crossroads.

3.1.3 Addressing the Question of Vulnerability

The tenets of distributive justice in the context of clinical research dictates that everyone, irrespective of gender, race or ethnicity, nationality or age, has an equal right to have medicines tested for them and on them. Risks and benefits should be evenly distributed among all groups. The exclusion of certain patient groups such as children, women and the elderly from research may stem from a desire to protect, but in fact may have the opposite effect in certain instances and can indeed put these vulnerable groups in harm's way. In essence, those deliberately excluded from research without sound reason are denied distributive justice. This resonates from the 'Draft National Ethical Guidelines for Biomedical and Health Research involving Human Participants, 2016' put out for public comments by the ICMR, where the term 'vulnerable population' was defined as:

> Those individuals who are relatively or absolutely incapable of protecting their own interests because of personal disability, environmental burdens or social injustice, lack of power, understanding or ability to communicate or are in a situation that prevents them from doing so.

And further goes on to say that,

> In general, these participants should be included in research only when the research is directly answering the health needs or requirements of the group. However, vulnerable populations have an equal right

---

14. The petition filed by the NGO Swasthya Adhikar Manch in the Supreme Court of India rests on this very conception that concurrent global drug development poses higher risks while drug lagged clinical development via bridging trials is a safer option and poses less harm (from personal communication with one of the stakeholders in the case).

to be included in research so that benefits accruing from the research apply to them too.

For instance children have traditionally been specifically excluded from clinical research, as they are considered too vulnerable, with the result that reliable evidence about the efficacy and safety of drugs used to treat them is limited or lacking. There has been a shift in the long-standing paradigm of protecting vulnerable participants from risk by excluding them from research. It is now recognised that, notwithstanding the risks, there are benefits for the participants involved in research. Eventually, in the case of research providing evidence on medicines, the benefit will include the possibility to prescribe medicines based on evidence, rather than off-label and this has been shown to be safer for the patients. In fact, it has been shown that children are better protected if treated according to a research protocol, than if receiving off-label prescriptions (Smyth and Weindling 1999). Legislation is now in place in the USA and the European Union (EU) to facilitate and encourage research in children, and indeed to mandate testing on children the new drugs that they may need. For developing countries, addressing vulnerability is of paramount importance, but the choice of modalities adopted may sometimes not be the optimal solution in the long run (see Section 4 for further elaboration).

In the backdrop of these paradoxes, several intricacies presented by the developing world can further complicate the already convoluted dynamics operating in the domain of clinical research. Usually CT programmes are formulated with the view to register the product as fast as possible. However, issues related to globalisation and ethical and scientific developments in developing countries have been raised in the recent past (Barry 1988, Angell 1988, Glickman et al. 2009, Thatte and Bavdekar 2008).

The ease of accessibility to regions with inadequate regulatory framework and largely unaware populations has raised questions on the unequal social contexts in which CTs are conducted. The increase in the number of CTs being conducted in these setups have brought about social, legal and ethical implications. Another criticism faced by the globalisation of trials has been the clear gap between the trials being conducted in developing regions and the availability of these new drugs. Till 2015 the total clinical trials with participation from CT sites in India and/or South Africa, 39.6 per cent and 60.1 per cent CTs in India and South Africa, respectively led to market authorisation in EU/US without a New Drug Application (NDA) approval in either India or South Africa (Limaye et al. 2015).

There are various risks associated with the conduct of CTs in developing countries. Literature points out that conducting CTs in the developing countries can at times, be an unethical practice as treatment- and politically-naïve population pools are more prone to 'therapeutic misconception' (Emanuel et al. 2004). The concerns are mainly related to the medical and social relevance of the studies in these geographies (Wendler et al. 2004), quality and symmetry of information in informed consents, exchange of updates of the trial results between participants and researchers, use of placebos versus standard of care, availability of the interventions to the participants pool after completion of the trials, and minimising risks during in the procedures involved in the conduct.

The less-developed countries have different attributes as compared to the developed world and relates to factors like lack of income and education, absence of knowledge about political powers and social representation, restricted access to information about the trials and their own health history and diverse customs and norms. Constrained by these factors, the risks involved in undertaking CTs in developing countries is higher (Lorenzo et al. 2010). A low level of schooling along with the absence of a public healthcare system, a common characteristic of low-income countries, leads to a higher risk of admission of patients uninformed about their own health records in the trials. This results in omission of information about prior clinical situations and any other knowledge that might adversely impact the patient under the drug treatment. Since, this would require additional scrutiny by researchers and involves high costs, such investigations are, at times, avoided.

The risk of involving participants in CTs from developing countries is increased by the inadequate healthcare facilities in these countries and questions the quality of equipment at these sites in cases of emergency and adverse events. The situation is further exacerbated when the ethical responsibility to provide a high standard of care to the trial participants is warranted, where none exists, compounding the ethical dilemma of using placebos in control groups.

In a nutshell, the socio-economic circumstances in the developing countries generate unforeseeable risks outside the purview of CTs protocols and the need for ethical conduct is being increasingly felt to factor these while deploying GCTs. The purpose of the CTs regulation is to protect the rights, safety and welfare of participants of CTs; to assure the fidelity of data produced by those trials and to align the administrative provisions governing their approval and oversight by NDRAs and ECs. The limited regulatory bandwidth with the NDRAs in developing countries to oversee the entire gamut of activities loosens this mandate, but does not take away from the significance of clinical research for a developing country like India while concomitantly making us think about how to do it more ethically.

3.2 Developing a Culture of Research and Innovation: The Clinical Research Perspective

The public value of the CTs and its results cannot be undermined. Once the findings of a CT are published and known, the use of the gained medical knowledge is manifold. Once the trials are formalised, the end-results, irrespective of the success, provide significant information to the scientists, sponsors, competing companies, drug regulators, and the final users of the drugs. The NDRAs review this data to check for the safety and efficacy of intervention; the academic journals need evidence to ensure that the published findings of the trials are reliable and unbiased; doctors and research professionals are in constant need of data to advance routine clinical practice and the patients get a glimpse of the data via the 'product labels' and in certain cases by giving informed consent for further exploratory/confirmatory studies (Rodwin and Abramson 2012). Further, evidence about the potential new molecules and drugs; drugs to be taken to the next phase of testing; procedures to efficiently use the drug and rational drug use are the positive externalities generated via CTs. The results on safety and therapeutics of drugs could also assist in follow-up innovation and work as a guidance to future research and researchers.

However, confidentiality of results benefits the pharmaceutical companies (which are the major funders for drug innovation) (Dorsey et al. 2010) to maintain a competitive edge, which helps maintain a healthy bottom line leading to funding further research for future products to sustain this cycle. It is becoming increasingly important in the ever competitive enterprise of drug discovery for researchers to develop innovative drug discovery strategies in order to fill their drug pipelines. More than being patient driven, novel drug discovery research is strategy driven. Fewer than 1 in 50 drug discovery projects results in the delivery of a single drug to the market (see Figure 3.6). The observed high attrition rate is unsustainable and researchers must constantly reassess their tactics in order to translate discovery research into clinical success. Tied to the success of a novel drug is the reputation, valuation, growth and revenue pipeline for a company. This is even more perilous for start-up biopharmaceutical firms, which largely rely on angel investors or venture funds and pin their hopes on a limited number of drug candidates, whose success can lead to a make or break moment for these firms. Almost two thirds of these investments are sunk into sustaining simultaneous clinical development programmes across the globe.

The most conservative estimate of the cost for bringing a single novel drug to the market is $161 million and the broadest figure stands at $2.4 billion (in 2015).[15] Given the high financial costs of conducting trials, novel drug discovery is highly dependent on the pharmaceutical industry. The non-profit agencies including 'academia' too in most cases has to seek industry or government support to translate their leads from the 'proof of concept stage' to the later stages of development. However, the business of novel drug development may not augur well with public health architecture, and the case may be more acute for disease profiles prevalent in most developing countries.[16] The limited success rate of drug development and the huge sunk costs limit abilities of most firms to undertake extensive global clinical programmes for diseases endemic to tropical countries, where a threadbare payer[17] structure offers little in terms of adequate return on investment.

But as corporations focus more on corporate sustainability efforts and social responsibility, their business models may expand to include more social goods in their day-to-day strategies and operations. Still in the current paradigm of novel

---

15. Examination of CT costs and barriers for drug development, task order no. HHSP23337007T (2014). Available at https://aspe.hhs.gov/report/examination-clinical-trial-costs-and-barriers-drug-development (Last accessed on 4 April 2017).

16. This has come to be known as the 10/90 Gap—the claim is that only 10 per cent of global health research is devoted to conditions that account for 90 per cent of the global disease burden. Exponents of the so-called 10/90 gap claim that the current pharmaceutical R&D paradigm results in too many resources being invested in the diseases of the rich at the expense of the poor. However, this concept has been criticised for grossly underplaying mortality and morbidity profiles of non-communicable diseases or life style diseases.

17. Payer, in health care, generally refers to entities other than the patient that finance or reimburse the cost of health services.

Figure 3.6

An Overview of the Drug Development Process

Preclinical		Clinical			Approval	Market
Toxicology	Investigational New Drug Application	Phase I	Phase II	Phase III	New Drug Application	Phase IV
		Safety	Safety Dosing Efficacy	Safety Efficacy Side effects		
Time		21.6 months	25.7 months	30.5 months		
1 to 6 years	6 to 11 years				0.6 to 2 years	11 to 14 years

Overall probability of success

30%   14%   9%   8%

Conditional probability of success

40%   75%   48%   64%   90%

Notes: The line marked "overall probability of success" is the unconditional probability of reaching a given stage. For example, 30 per cent of drugs make it to phase I testing. The line marked "conditional probability of success" shows the probability of advancing to the next stage of the process conditional on reaching a given stage. For example, the probability of advancing to Phase III testing conditional on starting Phase II testing is 48 per cent.

Source: Dimasi et al. (2003).

drug development, the economic reality is that privately supplied social goods, in this case, relevant clinical trial data, continues to be underprovided. The under-providence here means that the economic transaction between private corporations and the society is not Pareto-optimal and the private sector typically does not produce these social goods in socially efficient quantities. In this case, the under-providence is translated into a skewed allocation of funds for clinical studies that caters to a limited disease burden in any given country/region. For example, 40 per cent of trials sponsored by foreign pharmaceutical firms in India are targeting diabetes (18%) and cancers/neoplasms (22%) respectively.[18] The meta-category of non-communicable diseases (NCDs) receive the maximum R&D focus: over 90 per cent of the trials sponsored by foreign MNCs; followed by 77 per cent trials sponsored by Indian pharmaceutical firms and over 70 per cent sponsored by non-profit agencies targeting NCDs (see Figure 3.7).

Although India, like many other developing nations is witnessing a triple burden of disease[19] and hence R&D for tackling NCDs is in India's long term interest. Yet considering the current mortality profiles for India, the 'communicable, maternal, perinatal and nutritional conditions' require immediate R&D focus. By virtue of being net receivers of this social good, the stakeholders in developing countries cannot dictate drug development tailored to their immediate needs.

Given these market distortions and the growing costs of CTs and overall drug development, it is pertinent to note that a passive bystander approach will only prolong the status quo of non-availability of drugs for certain disease categories. The ability to hone a captive clinical research milieu allows for a socially-efficient availability of products (new drugs) and the information related to the products. Research involving 'from the molecule to man.' not only benefits the health of the nation but is also important economically.

The state is primarily responsible for the health of individuals within their jurisdiction as a tenet

---

18. This is not to suggest that these diseases are irrelevant to the Indian setting, but merely to showcase that certain therapeutic categories receive greater thrust from pharmaceutical companies.

19. For a better exposition, see Mehdi et al (2016).

Figure 3.7
Registered Trials in India: Disease Category-Sponsor Profile

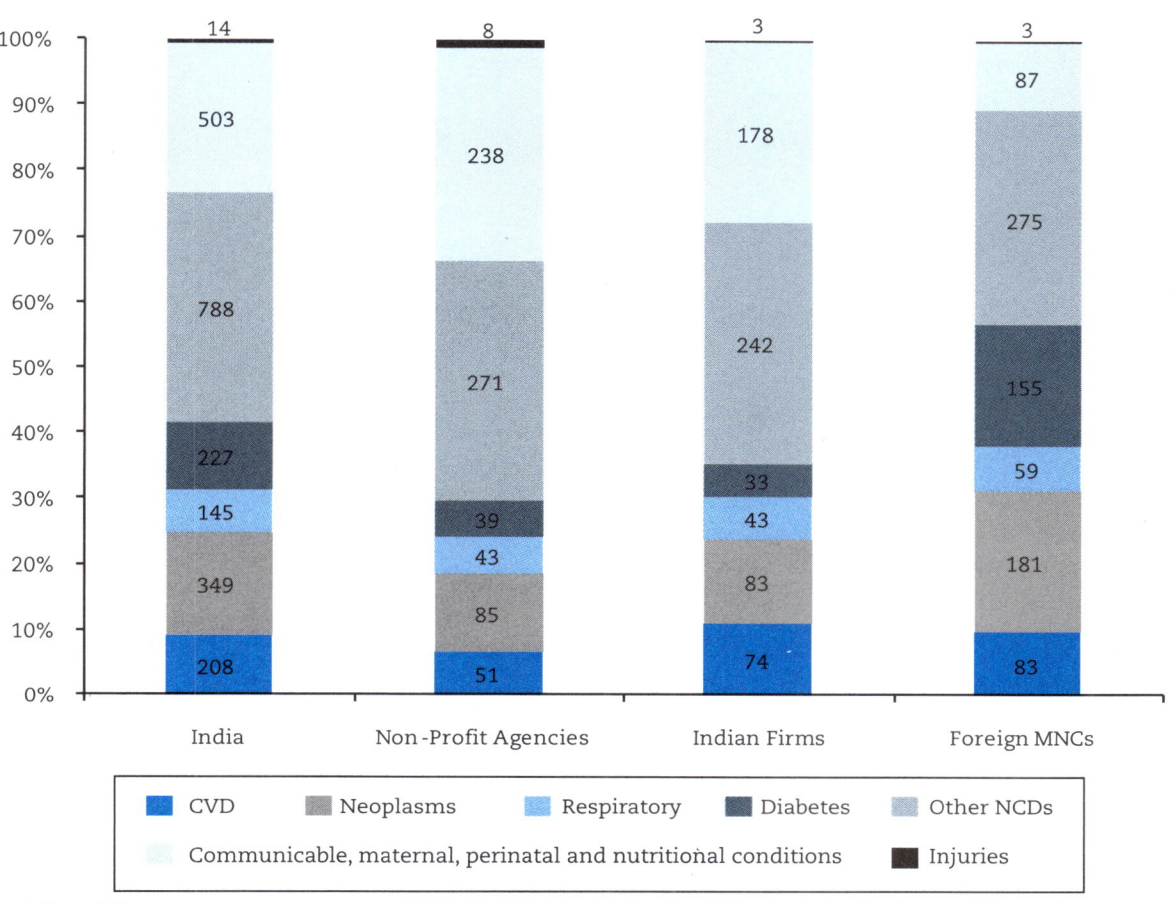

Source: Compiled from CTRI Dataset.

of justice (Pratt et al. 2012). This not only entails providing the best health infrastructure in the country but also permitting health research tailored for their countries. Partaking in the studies will help increased access to drugs and therapeutics for the health needs of the country. With such an arrangement, the host country and its government will have an obligation to prioritise hosting of those research projects that cater to the disease burden in the host country. Such an integration is advantageous because it encourages clinically relevant trials to be instituted in the country to maximise overall social welfare. According to Mazzetti et al. (2012), it is important to promote the development of CTs by state-affiliated institutions and universities, research centres and hospitals to meet the health ends in the country, including development of orphan drugs and neglected diseases, and therapeutic use of native resource.

Ensuring clinical research programmes meet the public health needs of a country is the rallying point in the entire debate on CTs.[20] Building an ecosystem for the ethical conduct of clinical research and clinically relevant trials is the most natural step forward.

3.3 Regulatory Landscape for Clinical Research of Countries in the Sample

Before the Nuremberg Code of 1947, human research was mostly self-regulated by researchers. The code established that ethical consideration and review are vital, and Declaration of Helsinki, 1964, noted that research protocols should be reviewed by an independent committee prior to initiation. In the USA, the National Research Act of 1974 established

---

20. CDSCO office order dated 5 September 2014 is key in this regard. See entry 17, in Appendix VII.

the National Commission for the Protection of Human Subjects of Biomedical and Behavioural Research. This commissioned the Belmont Report to make clear the ethical principles on which human research should be based. In 1981, the Department of Health and Human Services (DHHS) and the United States Food and Drug Administration (USFDA) issued regulations based on it. The Department of Health and Human Services issued the Code of Federal Regulations Title 45 (public welfare), Part 46 (protection of human subjects), and the FDA issued the Code of Federal Regulations Title 21 (food and drugs), Parts 50 (protection of human subjects) and 56 (Institutional Review Boards).

ICH and other GCP guidelines all state the need for ethical review by an impartial committee, known in some countries as institutional review boards. In the UK, as in other countries, the development of ECs from the late 1960s was rather ad hoc. Their the department of health issued a guidance for the formation of local ECs in 1991, and for multicentre ECs, in order to give ethical approval for studies at multiple sites, in 1997. In 2001, the National Research Ethics Service published Governance Arrangements for Research Ethics Committees and allowed for the streamlining of applications. This was updated in 2011. Other countries developed their own guidance and legislation, and the EU member states have been bound since 2004 by the European Clinical Trials Directive (Article 3 2a, Article 6), which superseded earlier guidance. The transposition into national law in different member states resulted in some differences in requirements for ECs, identified and quantified by the European Forum for good clinical practice. The Forum's report "The Procedure for the Ethical Review of Protocols for Clinical Research Projects in Europe and Beyond", updated in 2010, quantifies these differences, and the Report on Data on Research Ethics Committees in Seven Countries outside Europe gives similar information on non-EU countries.

The primary aim of all the regulations and codes is to safeguard the rights, safety and well-being of trial participants, and to facilitate good, well-planned and well-executed scientific research. They need to imbibe the tenets of distributive justice, and to stay free from political, institutional or market influences. Against this backdrop, key elements of the regulatory framework dictating clinical research in the countries under study are described here.

INDIA

Introduction

India's pharmaceutical industry has grown tremendously over the last few decades especially in the production of high quality and low cost generic drugs. It is estimated that the Indian pharmaceutical industry is likely to grow at 20 per cent compound annual growth rate (CAGR) over the next five years. However, an important characteristic of the pharmaceutical sector is its highly fragmented nature,[21] hence only a handful of firms are capable of instituting a full-fledged drug development programme. The hope was that as foreign firms conduct clinical research in the country, the homegrown firms would eventually catch up in this domain.

As already discussed, several changes since the turn of the millennium resulted in portraying India as a favourable destination for conducting clinical research. But the pace of regulatory change among other things rendered an altered global perception about India and the drug regulatory milieu at large.

The interviews across the countries reflected a common perception about India. On the positive side, a majority of the stakeholders across the board were of the view that India is an ideal location for conducting CTs as it has all the prerequisites required to develop a robust clinical research ecosystem. The biggest factor that contributes to this perception is the presence of a big treatment naïve population pool with defined epidemiological trends in certain therapeutic categories.

Interestingly, it was also pointed out that since the density of hospitals is on the lower side in India, a large number of patients may be dependent on a single hospital site. This makes a case for higher recruitment in trials along with a better prospect for clinical care for participants, given that the hospital ensures an infrastructure conducive for the conduct of CTs.

However, there were negative perceptions about the clinical research environment in India especially due to lack of a stable and predictable regulatory environment. According to a majority of the stakeholders, the ad-hoc nature of regulations has led India to remain an underdog in the domain of global clinical research. Most were unaware about

---

21. See, *https://www.ibef.org/industry/pharmaceutical-india.aspx* (Last accessed on 4 April 2017).

the specific regulatory changes brought in by the NDRA. For instance, most stakeholders especially those in European countries were unaware about the existence of the provisions relating to audio visual recording of informed consent.

On the academic front, it was found that although the universities abroad are interested to collaborate with Indian counterparts, a dedicated point of contact that could cater to queries regarding CTs was missing in Indian universities. This makes it difficult for potential foreign partners to collaborate with Indian researchers and physicians for trials. Besides, any foreign collaboration that results in attracting international funding for the conduct of clinical studies, has to go through the additional layer of regulation by the Health Ministry's Screening Committee (HMSC) housed in the Indian Council for Medical Research (ICMR). It was reported that this additional step may add at least 6 months to the overall process as this is done as a serial process i.e. in case of a regulatory study, once HMSC grants approval to an application, only then can an Indian investigator file the application to the office of DCG(I), if required.

Perceptions about CDSCO

Several stakeholders were of the view that inconsistency in final approvals has been a weakness of Indian regulations. Further, the change in the law about indemnity (compensation for injury/death related to clinical trial)[22] was reported to be a major concern. It was suggested that CDSCO should be more predictable and transparent with its timelines and approvals and device a better communication strategy which is perceivably missing. This is in line with the recommendations of Prof Ranjit Roy Chowdhury Committee.

The Regulatory Framework for Clinical Research

Overview of the Clinical Trial Review Process

The review and approval process in India has been undergoing considerable alterations over the past few years. The NDACs which was established in 2011 has been renamed SECs. SEC members are chosen at random from a pool of experts and are mostly academicians working as consultants for the NDRA.

---

22. For better exposition, refer to section 4 of this report.

In September 2014, it was decided by an executive order that all new CT applications are to be evaluated as per the following criteria:

- Assessment of risk versus benefit to the patients.
- Innovation vis-à-vis existing therapeutic options.
- Unmet medical need in the country.

A three tier process was instituted for granting a CT approval. Firstly, all CT applications and new drugs are examined by the SECs, which gives its recommendations that are then assessed by the Technical Review Committee (TRC). This TRC is composed of experts from various therapeutic areas and has been constituted under the Directorate General of Health Services (DGHS). CT approval and new drug approvals are granted by the DCGI on the basis of the recommendations given by the TRC. The Hon'ble Supreme Court of India mandated that a system be established to supervise CTs by constituting an Apex Committee under the Chairmanship of the Secretary of Health and Family Welfare, which constitutes the final layer for a CTA (see Appendix VI).

Observation

> Most stakeholders said that the three tier review system has provided more transparency. In practice, this meant that reasons are now provided for all decisions, which can be accessed online via the minutes of the meetings of all these committees. However, at the same time majority of the stakeholders complained about the delays the new system is causing. Further many casted aspersions on the sustainability of the model running indefinitely, as this was done largely to assuage the Supreme Court orders.

The DCGI approval and EC approvals are to be compulsorily obtained before a sponsor can initiate a clinical trial except in case of CTs being conducted for non-regulatory/academic purposes.

Observation

> The minimum turnaround time for a CTA for a Phase 3 (from CDSCOs end) was reported to be >12 weeks and above and varies depending upon the protocol, therapeutic category and other factors.

Ethics Committee Approval

The review and approval process by DCG(I) and the EC review are both conducted parallel to each other, except in the case of CTs for academic/research purposes that are non-regulatory in nature. Most ECs are based at clinical or academic institutions and hospitals. Independent ECs also exist which basically function outside institutions and are allowed to review only bioavailibility/bioequivalence (BA/BE) protocols.

Observation

> Out of all the countries in the sample, this provision was found to be unique only for India. Several stakeholders in India that were part of legitimate independent ECs, registered frustration at the broad brushed restriction.

There are a total of 1,080 registered ECs with CDSCO (as on 1 August 2016)—836 of them are institutional ECs, while the rest 243 were independent ECs. Very few of the registered ECs are however accredited.[23]

Observation

> The huge number of ECs with only finite CT protocols to review per year was pointed as a cause of concern and an impediment to build institutional memory.
>
> A major concern raised was about GCP training of EC members and the accreditation of the ECs at large. The team interviewed a few EC members, who reported that trainings provided were either inadequate and in a few cases existed only on records.

An academic CT for a new indication or route of administration or new dose or dosage of an already approved drug formulation are not required to take approval from DCG(I) provided that the following conditions are satisfied:

- EC approves the trial; and
- the data generated is not intended for submission to the licensing authority.

The DCGI has to be intimated about the academic trials approved by the EC and about the possible overlap, if any. If no response is received to the EC by the DCGI within 30 days, it is to be presumed that such an approval is not required.

Observation

> Many academicians interviewed in India were not sure about the CTA policy on academic trials.[24] This was despite the fact that GSR 313 (E) dated 16 March 2016 was available in the public domain. Only after the several public appearances from various representatives from the office of DCG(I), did this exemption was made clear.

Each trial site has to be granted separate approval and the same must be informed to the DCG(I), after which a trial can be initiated. Any changes or proposals to add site(s) and investigator(s) to an already existing trial have to be approved by the EC and the DCG(I) should also be informed. If the DCG(I) does not respond to the said changes, it is presumed that the same is accepted by them.[25]

Procedural Norms in Clinical Research

Several amendments to CT regulations under the D&C Rules were introduced in 2013 and later. The objective was to improve patient safety, reporting timelines of serious adverse events including deaths during CTs, and the payment of compensation to patients, etc. The amendment resulted in several concerns for researchers and research organisations around the areas of financial compensation and liability of the trial researchers. A few key issues are discussed below:

1) Insurance and Indemnity Clauses

As per the Indian GCPs and the ICMR Guidelines, the sponsor has to provide insurance coverage for any unforeseen injury to research participants. Prior to the commencement of a trial, a CT agreement by a sponsor has to specifically deal with the issues relating to indemnity and insurance between them or a CRO and the investigator or an institution. As per Schedule Y, a copy of the insurance has to be submitted to the EC while seeking approval.

---

23. The National Accreditation board for hospitals and Healthcare Providers (NABH), Quality council of India, has been mandated to develop a system of accreditation for ECs. MoHFW vide a letter dated 28 November 2016 to DCG(I), accorded approval for accreditation of ECs involved in supervision of CTs mandatory from 1 January 2018. Prior to that accreditation was voluntary, however now it is now conjectured that from 1 January 2018, only accredited ECs will be able to approve CTs.

24. See entry 25, in Appendix VII.

25. CDSCO published a circular in August 2016 providing that clinical trial sponsors no longer must obtain a NOC from DCGI each time they add a site or investigator to a study. See Circular, No. 12-01/14DC (Pt-47), CDSCO (August 3 2016), available at: http://www.cdsco.nic.in/writereaddata/noc.pdf (Last accessed on 4 April 2017).

> **Case Study 1**
>
> **Capacity Building in Ethics Committees**
>
> The Forum for Ethics Review Committees in India (FERCI) is a registered society and represents the India chapter of the larger umbrella organization called the Forum for Ethics Review Committees in Asia Pacific (FERCAP). It has established a network of Ethics Committees (ECs) in India and has been contributing to training and awareness regarding research ethics through various initiatives. One of the noteworthy initiatives is the CREaTe—FERCI initiative. Under the programme five IT enabled tools have been created to facilitate the day to day functions of ECs. The five tools are:
>
> 1. Simplifier: It is a database of key terms commonly seen in consent forms that are "simplified". The jargons from the discipline of medicine are explained in simpler terms for a literate lay person to comprehend.
>
> 2. Interpreter: It is a database that has validated simple "interpretations" of terms commonly found in consent forms. At present this database has Marathi and Hindi interpretations. It is not a mere transliteration tool and derives its value because it is a compendium of words put together by brute force translation, which can go a long way to guide trial participants.
>
> 3. EthiX: It is a self-assessment tool to evaluate the ethical soundness of a clinical study protocol and an informed consent document. Scores are assigned on the basis of the responses of the scientific as well as ethical questions designed for different study designs. It is a user guided questionnaire based tool that scores a protocol based on its ethical soundness.
>
> 4. Regulert: It is a feed based free subscription service, which notifies the subscribers about relevant notifications and other information from various stakeholders including CDSCO, USFDA, EMA, MHRA, Health Canada, WHO etc.
>
> 5 eEC: This tool enables institutions to move their Ethics Committees review and approval practices on to the CReATE Platform. Once on board, investigators can register with an institute and submit their studies/projects for Institutional Ethics Committee (IEC) approval. Once these are submitted to IEC, they will go through IEC staff verification and IEC members review and approval/rejection of project/submission.
>
> Under the pilot, over 30 ECs have been trained which are now named "Smart ECs", and the list is growing. The pilot is in its infancy, yet has been able to establish proof-of-concept, which is scalable for a pan-India implementation. All the tools combined together serve a much needed function, and can go a long way to rectify challenges affecting clinical research in India. Similar initiatives in other countries have only enhanced the capacity of ECs. For example: Council on Health Research for Development (COHRED) created an online platform 'Research for Health and Innovation Organiser' (RHInnO), which provides researchers with access to an easy to use automated system that enables them to keep track of the entire life-cycle of the research process. RHInnO enables users, researchers and research institutions to register research projects, issue calls for proposals and manage research data and publish research results. The 'ethics' version of RHInnO enables ECs to streamline the ethics review process, produce reports and track the progress of projects. One of the ECs interviewed confirmed the merits of deploying the online platform.

In India, usually a sponsor enters into an indemnity agreement with the CRO, investigator or institution which covers any risks related to study-related injuries due to any act, omission, negligence or misconduct by the CRO, investigator or institution. An insurance cover has to be procured to cover any costs incurred due to this indemnification.

Insurance in India is to be issued by a local insurance company.

Observation

> Currently, the recommended coverage is about 10 million rupees (Although no EC member interviewed was able to comment about how the adequacy of the insurance coverage was judged or ensured).

Although many Indian subsidiaries of multinational pharmaceutical companies also get insured under the insurance programmes of the parent company, it is important to also obtain insurance from a local company since insurance policies issued abroad are considered illegal in India.

Observation

> It was reported by several stakeholders that due to reputational effects and other factors, in most instances, compensations are paid directly by the sponsor and formal claims from the insurance companies are rarely pressed for.

Investigator driven research in medical institutions relies on institutional insurance covers.

Observation

> There were mixed opinions on the conditions an insurance cover was required. Most academicians interviewed demanded a guidance to be issued in this regard.

2) Compensation for Participation; Injury and Death

As per the Indian GCP Guidelines; the ICMR Guidelines and the D&C Rules, 1945, before a trial begins, a sponsor has to agree in a CT agreement to provide medical treatment as well as to provide compensation to the participants, in case of any physical or mental injury occurring during a trial.[26] As per the recent amendments, medical treatment has to be provided for as long as it is needed or till the time it is proved that the injury is not due to CT participation. In case there is no permanent injury, compensation should be paid accordingly along with the loss of wages. If an injury or death is identified at a later stage of the study and is established to be drug-related, the sponsor has to provide compensation.

As per the amended Rule 122 DAB, a sponsor has to compensate a participant and/or his/her legal heir(s) if the injury or death has occurred due to any of the following reasons:

- adverse effects of investigational product(s) (IPs);
- any clinical trial procedures involved in the study;
- violation from approved protocol, scientific misconduct or negligence by the investigator/sponsor/CRO, or other responsible parties;
- failure of an IP to provide intended therapeutic effect where, the standard of care, though available, was not provided to the participant as per trial protocol;
- use of a placebo in a placebo-controlled trial where, the standard of care, though available, was not provided to the participant as per trial protocol;
- adverse effects due to concomitant medication administered as per the approved protocol;
- injury to the child in-utero due to a parent's participation in a clinical trial.

The participant may be compensated for his/her time spent, for the expenses incurred. He/she may also receive medical treatment for free- related to his/her participation till the time the same is required.

A local CRO or a representative may be appointed in case of a foreign sponsor. There should be an agreement between the foreign sponsor and the local representative, giving responsibility to the latter for the medical treatment of the participant as well as providing any financial compensation in case of any injury or death resulting from the trial.

The latest amendment states that it is the responsibility of the sponsor to report any serious AEs (SAEs)/ serious ADRs (SADRs) within 14 days of its occurrence to the DCGI and the EC that had given its approval to the study. This EC has to give its recommendations with respect to the compensation within a period of 30 days to the DCGI after which the DCGI will determine the cause of injury/death and determine the quantum of compensation within 150 days of occurrence of the event. Within 30 days of the compensation order by the DCGI, the sponsor is supposed to pay compensation to the participant or his/her legal heir. In 2013, the CDSCO came out with a compensation formula in case of death and in December 2014, the CDSCO came out with a formulae to determine the quantum of compensation in case of CT related injury (other than death). With these formulas in place, India becomes the only country to do so for the purpose of providing compensations for injuries or death related to trial.

---

26. However, an analysis for relatedness is conducted for the purpose of disbursing a compensation. The choice of words "during" the rule and the practice followed on ground leads to further confusion.

Observation

> From the field, it emerged that the stakeholders from the industry in India fully supported the formulae while others mentioned that it is too early to gauge the impact. The often cited reason for support was the upper limit in the quantum of compensation and hence the certainty the formulas brings in case of providing compensations for injury or death.

In case a sponsor does not provide for compensation, the DCGI may, after a show-cause notice to the sponsor, pass a written order to either suspend or cancel the trial and may also restrict the sponsor/CRO or representative of a foreign sponsor to conduct any further trials in India.

Ethical Norms in Clinical Research

Informed Consent Process

To conduct a CT in India, the participant has to give a written consent, which is in compliance with all the requirements in the Indian GCP, the ICMR Guidelines and Schedule Y. As per these guidelines, an informed consent form (ICF) and a patient information sheet are to be approved by the EC and then the DCGI. A trial can commence only after these documents are approved. The investigator has to provide all information related to the trial to the participant as well as to a witness. This information should be in both written as well as in oral form and in clear and understandable terms. Verbal consent may also be taken from a participant in case a signature or thumb impression is not possible. In such a case, verbal consent may be taken in presence of a witness or through an audio/video means. However, in 2015, the D&C Rules were amended stating that in case of a trial of new chemical entity or new molecular entity for vulnerable participants, an investigator has to obtain an audio-visual recording of the informed consent process.

The contents of the ICF should be brief and clear and there should be no undue influence or coercion to enroll a participant in a trial. As per the ICMR Guidelines, if there is any change in the ICF due to reasons such as modification of the protocol or any alteration in the procedure, treatment or site, it has to be approved by the EC and then the DCGI. If this happens, the participant will have to resign and give his/her reconsent.

The participant and the investigator both have to sign and date the ICF. If the participant is illiterate, an impartial witness should be chosen who will sign and date the form after understanding the ICF. The signature to the form is the proof that the informed consent was given freedom and that the participant has understood everything and given his/her assent thereto.

USA

The Regulatory Framework for Clinical Research

Overview of the Clinical Trial Review Process

The United States Food and Drug Administration (USFDA) is the regulatory body that approves the use of the Investigational New Drug (IND) application. IND is "notice of claimed investigational exemption for a new drug," which is basically a request for 'exemption from the legal requirement that prohibits unapproved drugs from being transported or distributed across state lines.'

According to the Code of Federal Regulations Title 21 CFR Part 312 and Guidance on IND Determination, the FDA does not require the sponsor to submit an IND application for CTs with human subjects under certain conditions, including certain investigations of marketed drugs and bioavailability studies. Whether an IND is needed to conduct a clinical investigation of a marketed drug primarily depends on the intent of the investigation and the degree of risk associated with the use of the drug in the investigation.

Observation from India

> The notification GSR 313 (E) dated 16 March 2016 by CDSCO for filing for a CTA in case of academic trials, only factors in the intent behind the investigation, while leaves the risk assessment to be done by the ECs.

The most important purpose of FDA reviewing an IND is to ensure the safety and rights of the participants during the study. FDA's review of Phase 1 submissions emphasises on the safety of investigations in phase 1 while phases 2 and 3 submissions comprise of an evaluation of the scientific quality of the investigations and the probability of that investigations yielding data that is able to meet the regulatory standards needed for a marketing approval. A CTA is deemed to be approved if the sponsor does not receive any further request for additional data within 30 days of its submission.

Ethics Committee Approval

As per 21CFR, for any study, an approval from the institutional ethics committee is necessary. In the US, institutional EC are referred to as the IRBs or the Institutional Review Boards. 21CFR defines an IRB as one type of independent EC, and has the same meaning as an independent review committee. It indicates that an IRB is any board, committee, or other group formally designated by an institution to review, approve the initiation of, and conduct the periodic review of biomedical research involving human subjects to ensure the protection of the rights and welfare of the human subjects. 21CFR defines an independent EC as a review panel responsible for ensuring the protection of the rights, safety, and well-being of human subjects involved in a clinical investigation and can provide adequate assurance of that protection.

Each EC in the US that reviews clinical investigations regulated by the FDA and each EC in the US that reviews clinical investigations intended to support applications for research or marketing permits for FDA-regulated products must register at a site maintained by department of health and human services (DHHS). All other ECs may register voluntarily. Currently, there are 4789 active registered ECs with Office for Human Resources Protection (OHRP) (also includes ECs of foreign origin which have a voluntary registration).

Observations

> Every EC member interviewed in USA had undergone a minimum 15 hour online GCP certification course, which had to be renewed every few years, reportedly 3 years.
>
> The role of independent review boards was emphasised in the overall EC reviews where they have successfully taken the role of assisting institutional review boards in managing their workload. It was reported that in the last decade or so, the independent boards have had a change in perception and are now looked at as legitimate partners in contributing to a review.

Insurance and Indemnity Clauses

As such, there are no regulatory requirements regarding insurance and indemnity, but every sponsor takes a voluntary insurance cover for every CT. Investigators take insurance cover for claims arising from malpractice or gross negligence.

Observation

> On several occasions it was reported that Insurance claims are hardly pressed for, as trial participants are usually covered by their own private insurance.

Compensation for Participation; Injury and Death

As per 21CFR, all information relating to compensation in case of any trial-related injury or death is to be provided to the participant and his/her legal heirs by the sponsor or his/her designated CRO. Information relating to available medical treatments in case of injuries etc. is also to be provided to the participant and his/her legal heirs. Participants can also be paid for being part of the study and this compensation is often considered as a 'recruitment incentive'.

At the time of the initial review, payment amounts are provided to the IRB by the sponsor or his/her designated CRO so that the latter can ensure that the same are adequate. The IRB also has to ensure that the method and timing of payments to the subjects are fair and reasonable.

Ethical Norms in Clinical Research

Informed Consent Process

In the US, legally effective informed consent of the subject or the subject's legally authorised representative has to be obtained in accordance with the conditions stipulated in 21CFR. 45CFR and 32CFR also state the requirements for informed consent. A form containing informed consent has to be approved by the IRB and the subject has to sign and date it. This form can be in written form or in a short form wherein the informed consent requirements have been explained verbally. It is further stated that any information given to the subject has to be in a language understood by him/her or their legal representatives. In case of an illiterate person, the consent form can be read out to them by the legally authorised representatives and then signed. In case consent form is presented orally, a witness has to be present and the EC has to approve the written summary provided to it. In case of any change in the protocol, the presently enrolled subjects are to be informed of the same but only in case if the change might alter the subjects consent.

A video tape recording of the consent interview is also recommended by USFDA in case of illiterate participants who can understand and comprehend spoken English but are physically unable to talk or write.

SOUTH AFRICA

The Regulatory Framework for Clinical Research

Overview of the Clinical Trial Review Process

The Medicines Control Council (MCC) is a statutory body that reviews and approves all CT applications for any new indications as per the General Regulations Made in Terms of the Medicines and Related Substances Act 101 of 196 (GRMRSA), the South African GCPs (SA-GCP). The MCC assesses all CTs from Phases 1-4 and BA/BE studies.

The secretariat to the MCC i.e. the Medicines Regulatory Authority (MRA) manages the CT application process. The MCC houses a Clinical Trials Committee (CTC) and the MRA renders all the administrative support to the CTC. The prime responsibility of the CTC is to consider both the scientific and ethical aspects of a CT application and to ensure that the application meets all the criteria relating to safety and efficacy.

Observation

> It was reported that a member from the CTC is assigned to every protocol, but the identity is blinded from the sponsor to avoid conflict of interests. The most common outcome of a CTA from the MCC was reported to be 2A or 2B (see Table 3.4).
>
> The minimum turnaround time for a CTA for a Phase 3 trial (from MCCs end) was reported to be more than 12 weeks which may be prolonged depending upon the protocol, therapeutic category and other factors.

Ethics Committee Approval

The National Health Research Ethics Council (NHREC) is the body advising the Department of Health (DoH) on health research ethics management and also states ethical norms and standards. As per Section 73 of the National Health Act 61 of 2003 (NHA), every institution, health agency, and health establishment where research is conducted has to institute an EC or should have access to an independent EC. The EC has to be registered with the NHREC.

Observation

> As on 1 August 2016, there are 44 registered ECs with the NHREC and 3 out of these were reported to be of independent origin.
>
> The independent ECs were reported to be of high caliber and respected across the board for their capacity to deliver unbiased reviews in a timely fashion. No out of ordinary mechanisms were in place to remove conflicts of interests.

As per the SA-GCPs, prior to commencement of any trial, the sponsor has to submit a CTA to both the MCC and a registered EC for approval. The sponsor or the PI has to register the trial information on the South African Human Research Electronic Application System website, after which the system generates an NHREC registration number. Thereafter, a South African National Clinical Trials Register (SANCTR) National Register Number is issued by the DoH within two working days and communicated to the EC as well as the sponsor/principal investigator.

Insurance and Indemnity Clauses

A sponsor has to provide insurance for injury and death resulting from trial to all the participants. As per the SA-GCPs, the sponsor has to follow the guidelines laid down in the Association of the British Pharmaceutical Industry (ABPI) guidelines. While submitting the CT application, an insurance certificate and indemnity also has to be submitted to the MCC. This certificate must include:

- references to the applicable regulatory and legal provisions;
- insurer company name;
- insurance policy number;
- name and address of the policy holder;
- study name, identification number, and protocol dates covered by the policy.

Compensation for Participation; Injury and Death

The MCCs CTC has recommended a minimum compensation of ZAR 50 per study visit to cover travel and incidental expenses incurred to the participant. In addition, the SA-GCP also mentions that the researcher has to account for participant travel and other expenses.

For compensation requirements also, the SA-GCPs recommends that the sponsor has to follow the ABPI's guidelines to comply with South Africa's participant compensation and treatment requirements due to trial-related injuries. As per these guidelines, the sponsor has to provide written assurance to the investigator to pay compensation to participants and/or legal heirs in case of any trial related injury or death. This information has to be communicated to the EC as well by the investigator.

The SA-GCPs lays down basic principles to be followed by the sponsors while paying compensation:

- a causal relationship should exist between a participant's injury and his/her participation in a trial;
- when a child is injured in utero through his/her mother's participation in a CT;
- when the injury results in permanent injury or disability to the participant;
- when there is an adverse reaction to a medicinal product under trial, and injury is caused by a procedure adopted to deal with that adverse reaction.

The amount of compensation to be paid should be apposite to the severity and the possibility of recurrence of the injury. The amount of damages awarded should be in tandem with the commonly awarded compensation for similar injuries.

Compensation paid could be reduced or excluded in case following conditions are satisfied:

- The seriousness of the disease being treated.
- The degree of likelihood that adverse reactions will occur.
- The risks and benefits of the established treatments relative to those known or suspected of the trial medicines.

In case there is a dispute as to the amount of compensation to be paid, the sponsor may seek opinion of an expert, who is mutually acceptable. The sponsor should consider the opinion of the expert before deciding on the amount of compensation to be made.

Any claims by the participant are to be made to the sponsor via investigator which the sponsor may review expeditiously.

Ethical Norms in Clinical Research

Informed Consent Process

In clinical trials in South Africa, consent form is to be signed by the participant according to the principles set out in the NHA, the Declaration of Helsinki, the SA-GCPs, and the ICH Harmonised Tripartite Guideline for GCP E6 (R1) (ICH-GCPs). The consent form has to be written and both this form and the patient information sheet are documents that are essential and are to be reviewed by the EC and thereafter submitted to the MCC along with the CTA.

The investigator has to provide all the necessary information pertaining to the trial to the participant and/or his/her legal representatives. The contents

Table 3.4
Clinical Trial Committee Classification of the Review of CTAs in South Africa

Classification	Comment	Items Outstanding
1A	Approved	No Items Outstanding
1B	Approved	1 item outstanding
2A	Not Approved. For approval by in house evaluators	1-2 or more items outstanding as deemed by the committee
2B	Not approved for approval by the original evaluator and in-house if the need arises	1-2 or more items outstanding as deemed by the committee
3	Not Approved	Items outstanding to come back to the next CTC meeting at the next cycle
4	Not Approved	For referral for specialist opinion
5	Not approved - technical/ scientific deficiencies	Not Approved – Applicant to resubmit for the next cycle.
6	Rejected	Administrative and technical items outstanding

Source: Clinical Trial Unit, Medicines Control Council, South Africa.

> **Case Study 2**
>
> **Speaking Books: An audio visual aid**
>
> *Idea*: A range of easy-to-use audio books designed to get potentially life-saving health messages out to clinical trial participants.
>
> *Problem*: In 2003, the South African Depression & Anxiety Group (SADAG)—country's largest mental health initiative, was horrified at how suicide rates among young South Africans were spiking. Mental health carries a huge social stigma across Africa and information booklets designed to help people with depression or mental health problems simply weren't working, especially in remote communities with high illiteracy rates. People weren't getting the help they needed—a 2009 study showed that only a quarter of the 16.5 per cent of South Africans suffering from mental health problems had received any kind of treatment.
>
> *Method*: Speaking books created a range of free books with simple audio buttons talking to the user through each page. The first speaking book, voiced by South African actress and celebrity Lillian Dube, was called 'Suicide shouldn't be a secret' and focused on how depression is a real and treatable illness, encouraging people to get help when they need it. Several other were later created in different languages enumerating what does participating in CTs entail.
>
> *Verdict*: Speaking books have now produced 62 titles in 24 different languages and are now used in 20 African countries across the continent. The books now tackle a number of critical healthcare issues outside of suicide prevention such as HIV and Aids, malaria, maternal health and clinical trials. Speaking books has also expanded to other countries and are being increasingly used as an audio visual aid for priming subjects entering CTs. They are usually deployed before a formal informed consent is taken.

of the consent form should be brief and clear and without coercion and undue influence for enrolling in a CT.

As per the SA-GCPs, both written and verbal consent has to be obtained. In case the participant is illiterate, and/or his or her legal representatives are illiterate—verbal consent can be provided in presence of a literate person and that person has to countersign the form. In case there are any new findings during the course of the trial, the same must be informed to the participant who may choose to either continue or withdraw from the study.

Observations

> The research team was informed of some interesting use of audio visual aids, usually used before an informed consent was used in South Africa for the purposes of priming a potential patient.

EUROPEAN UNION

Europe has been a centre for research and development of pharmaceutical drugs and conduct of CTs. As of January 2016, there have been about 28, 971 trials being conducted in the EU region.

The Directive 2001/20/EC of the European Commission[27] (further referred to as the Directive) lays down the basic requirements for the conduct of CTs in the European Union (EU) and aims to harmonise the rules for the approval of a clinical trial conducted in a member state in the EU. Although the timelines and the basic structure of the approvals is outlined by the Directive, the member states follow discretion in the how it is implemented. The impact of the directive is summarised based on observations from two countries i.e. UK and Germany, which have had markedly different modes of authorising clinical research.

Prior to the Directive, there was no expression of the provision of clinical trial authorisation in UK, rather the supply of the investigational product for clinical research needed regulatory authorisation. The Medicines Act, 1968[28] controlled the sale and

---

27. Directive 2001/20/EC of the European Parliament and of the Council of 4 April 2001 on the approximation of the laws, regulations and administrative provisions of the member states relating to the implementation of GCP in the conduct of CTs on medicinal products for human use (Clinical Trials Directive).
28. See, The Medicines for Human Use (Clinical Trials) Regulations 2004 (*http://www.legislation.gov.uk/uksi/2004/1031/pdfs/uksi_20041031_en.pdf*) (Last accessed on 4 April 2017).

supply of the medicines and defined CTs as a study in patients looking at efficacy, thereby keeping the trials on healthy volunteers out of regulatory purview. Previously, many sponsors either applied for a CTC or notified the authority under the Clinical Trial Exemption (CTX) or the Doctors and Dentists Exemption (DDX) scheme.[29] With the Directive being adopted by the UK, these exemptions were discontinued and both commercial and non-commercial research had to apply for a clinical trials authorisation. The introduction of the Directive led to the inclusion of all types of interventional trials under the purview of regulatory authorities.

In Germany, prior to 2004, the applicants had to notify the competent authority about the trials and with revisions in German Law, a CT of a medicinal product on human beings could only be started by the sponsor if the competent regulatory authority and an EC had issued a favourable opinion on it.

As part of the EU, the Directive mandated the introduction of the Investigational Medicinal Product Dossier (IMPD), a single document that had to be submitted to the competent authorities in the UK and Germany for approval of a CT. Although this improved the collection of data and ethical standards at work along with giving practical timelines for approvals, the Directive increased the administrative burden and costs of CTs for both pharmaceutical companies as well as academic research.[30]

Ethics Review in EU

The ethics review of the clinical trial protocol in Europe is simultaneously done alongside the regulator's review of the CTs application. No CT can be initiated prior to the approval by the ECs and the regulatory agency. The Directive outlines the establishment and working of ECs in its member states to oversee the ethical aspect of the protocols, and comment and ask for modifications in the protocols whenever necessary. The ECs have a maximum of 60 days from the date of receipt of a valid application to give its reasoned opinion to the applicant and the competent authority in the member state concerned (Article 6, Directive 2001/20/EC). The formal structure of the ECs, registrations, qualifications, extent of responsibilities is decided by the member states.

The UK follows a centralised registration procedure for its ECs called the Research Ethics Committees (RECs). These are formally institutionalised under the National Research Ethics Service (NRES). Only one REC approval is required for single (or multi) centre trials conducted in the UK; an additional site-specific assessment (SSA) may be necessary for trials with non-NHS sites. Since the country follows a central system, the RECs are not affiliated to any individual institution and need to establish written standards operating procedures (SOPs). The process of submission of protocol to the EC is electronic and it takes around 30-days for an approval excluding the time for additional information is sought from the applicant. However, for early-phase trials, the review time is quickened and the applicants are allowed to pre-book slots closer to the meeting date of the REC. In order to keep up with the advancements at work, the members of the RECs are required to do a one-day training per year and the type of training can vary according to the type of CTs reviewed by them.

On the other hand, in another EU country, Germany, the structure and functioning of the ECs is entirely different. Germany follows a decentralised system of ethical review and has different kinds of ECs— affiliated with universities, medical agencies in the states and the regional EC of a state. If the investigator has private practice and is not involved with any university, then permission for the trial has to be taken from the regional EC in his country. Apart from this, there are two categories of ECs in a CT in Germany. An EC called the main or coordinating EC, located where the lead investigator of the CT is situated; and ECs referred to as nodal ECs, situated at the site level, where the trial is being run. The latter only have the capacity to comment on the qualifications of the site and not on the scientific and ethical aspects of the protocol. Due to the different ECs involved in the approval of a single trial, the timeline is stretched as compared to the UK and somewhat varies across the different states of Germany.[31]

In some ECs, the investigator is invited for the EC meetings for quicker query resolutions. Unlike various other member states, there are no formal laws guiding how the ECs should work, or the qualifications of the members and therefore, there

---

29. See, Controls on the Conduct of Clinical Trials in United Kingdom, *The Textbook of Pharmaceutical Medicine* (2013).
30. Ibid.
31. On an average, the single-centre trials take around 15-20 days whereas the multi-centre trials take 45-60 days for approvals.

is discretion in the way applications are studied at different sites. This, at times, makes it difficult for the applicants to plan how their CTA is assessed given the heterogeneity of requirements and assessments. Further, the fee varies between ECs and the regularity in meeting is different for different ECs. Although there is no legal requirement for training for EC members, the Permanent Working Party of German Research Ethics Committees has established formats for one-day training for EC members.

All the countries follow GCP guidelines as per the Directive and have training for GCP as well. Further, both the countries have provisions for taking expert opinion from an external source on complex protocols. In the UK, the regulatory agency provides advice to the ECs under a Memorandum of Understanding within 48 hours of a query being raised. In Germany, seeking external expertise is compulsory for trials with 'gene therapeutics', and in pediatrics with no EC specialists.

Compensation and Insurance

Most of Europe follows the universal health system with the public insured for health benefits. In any case, the people do not directly pay for their own healthcare, and therefore, the need for an additional insurance only arises from an event during a clinical trial that is related to any damage that alters the quality of life for these populations.

Several initiatives have been made to improve the clinical research environment in European countries. The UK regulatory authorities have certain scientific advice procedures as well an innovation office and provide advice to the small and medium companies along with information on intricate protocols. It has been trying to attract early phase trials in the country with quicker decisions on trial protocols and have various inspection schemes depending on the risks involved with these trials. In Germany, the federal funds have been utilised for further development of the research environment. In the EU, unmet medical needs and niche areas of research have received support in form of the orphan drug legislation and has been implemented rigorously.

However, the growth in the number of CTs being conducted around the world and the need for better medications have put pressure on existing sites in developed countries. The state-of-the art infrastructure in some of the sites in the UK and Germany has increased the costs of carrying out trials primarily because of high human capital costs. This, in turn, has led to a shift of the trial sites to cheaper locations like Eastern Europe. Further, in Germany, the decentralisation of the ECs has led to increased bureaucracy at work and delayed approvals for multi-centre trials. Further details of countries specific regulations are described below:

UNITED KINGDOM

In the UK, there active funding in healthcare research has enabled several initiatives to positively influence the clinical research milieu. One such initiative has been the UK Clinical Research Collaboration (UKCRC)[32] which aims to improve the research environment in the UK by bringing the major stakeholders to clinical research at a single platform.

Observation

> One of the major concerns for UKCRC is the shift of trials from the UK to other parts of the world.

The central agency responsible for reviewing, assessing and approving CTAs in the UK is the Medicines and Healthcare Products Regulatory Agency (MHRA) which regulates and licenses all medicines and medical devices within the UK, and is responsible for CT approvals, inspections and oversight. The agency's clinical trials unit is specifically focused on reviewing applications to conduct CTs of medicinal products. Any CTA is deemed to be approved if no query is raised within 30 days of the receipt of a valid and complete CTA, virtually establishing a notification system. For Phase I trials, the MHRA has shortened the timeline while following the same procedure of examination. The CTU team comprises of a pharmaceutical assessor, toxicologist, non-clinical and clinical assessors who review an application in tandem. Further, any first-in human study is also assessed by a multi-disciplinary team. If the investigational product is classified as 'high risk', MHRA has the facility to seek expert advice from an advisory group of the commission for human medicines (CHM).

---

32. Established in 2004, the partnership brings together the major stakeholders that influence clinical research in UK- the research funding bodies, academia, the NHS, regulatory bodies, the bioscience, healthcare and pharmaceutical industries, and patients groups. One of the major concerns for the initiative was the shift of CTs from UK to other parts of the world.

Observation

> The additional stress on Phase 1 Trial was reportedly become of the unfortunate TeGenero (TGN1412) Trial.[33]

The Regulatory Framework for Clinical Research

Overview of the Clinical Trial Review Process

As per the Medicines for Human Use (clinical trials) Regulations, 2004 (MHCTR), review and approval process by MHRA is conducted in parallel with the EC's review. Approval by MHRA is conditional and contingent on the EC approval and vice versa. Eventually, the sponsor or his/her representative has to apply for a EudraCT number by registering a clinical trial in the EudraCT database.

Once a CTA is submitted, the MHRA's Information Processing Unit conducts an administrative validation within 10 days. An acknowledgment letter is sent once the application is validated. The MHRA's CTU assessment period begins from the date of receipt (Day 0) of a valid application. If the sponsor or his/her designated representative does not receive a request for additional information from the MHRA within 30 days, the CTA is treated as authorised.

Ethics Committee Approval

The UK Health Department has a centralised registration process for its ECs, commonly referred to as RECs. The authority responsible for coordinating the development of operational systems for ECs 'recognised' on behalf of the UK Ethics Committee Authority (UKECA), or 'authorised' on behalf of each of the four UK nations' (England, Northern Ireland, Scotland, Wales) Health Departments and their corresponding Research Ethics Service head offices is the NRES. The type of EC responsible for approval depends on the type of research being conducted.

Only one EC (main EC) review is required to be obtained by the NRES irrespective of the number of sites in the UK. For multi-centre CTs with sites outside the NHS system, a SSA may be necessary. Assessment forms that are site specific are to be submitted to the 'main EC' which confirms approval of each non-NHS site as part of its ethical opinion.

Observation from India

> The process varies from India where individual institutional ECs have to review and approve a CT protocol before it is initiated at their respective site. Various stakeholders suggested lack of experts at the local level for effective evaluation as a drawback for local EC approval. One EC may not have experts for all therapeutic areas and might not be able to assess a complicated CT at the local level.

Insurance and Indemnity Clauses

As per the MHCTR, it is legally required that insurance and indemnity provisions are to be made in order to cover the liability of the investigator and sponsor for injuries due to the trial. Even though it is not specifically stated, but it is the sponsor or his/her designated representative who is responsible to ensure that adequate insurance and indemnity is in place to cover the sponsor and investigators liability. These documents are also to be submitted while making a CTA.

Compensation for Participation; Injury and Death

In the UK, the compensation for any adverse event has been proactively defined by the ABPI rules and depend on the type of the trial and the event. If it is commercially-sponsored, then the sponsor uses its insurance policy for claims by participants. If it is non-commercial, then the event is covered by various indemnities. The clinical investigators have individual indemnity covers; indemnity covered by the NHS hospital and indemnity by NHS itself. If the conclusion is undeceive or unacceptable to the parties involved, it resorts to the tort laws.

The sponsor or his/her designated representative is responsible to provide compensation to research participants and/or their legal heirs in the event of Phase I trial-related injuries or death as per the requirements of MHCTR.

For compensation and treatments due to phase I related in injuries, the sponsor has to follow the ABPI's guidelines. As per these guidelines, the sponsor has to provide a written assurance to the investigator that he will provide for compensation to participants and/or his/her legal heirs in case of any trial related injury or death. This information is then provided to the relevant ECs by the investigator.

The sponsor or his/her designated representative must provide the details of insurance for each trial to

---

33. It was a first in human study where the trial volunteers faced catastrophic systemic organ failure. This was despite being administered at a supposed sub-clinical dose some 500 times lower than the dose found safe in animals.

the main EC using the statement of insurance cover form which requires the following information:

- Aggregate limit of the sponsor's indemnity for the trial and for the individual participant (it is recommended that sponsors purchase a minimum for £ 5 million indemnity cover for any first-in-human phase 1 trial, or £ 2.5 million for other phase 1 trials).

- Policy type (trial-specific or block), length, exclusions or other conditions.

- Insurer's name and address.

- Copy of insurance certificate.

Ethical Norms in Clinical Research

Informed Consent Process

As per the requirements set forth in the MHCTR, the ICH Harmonised Tripartite Guideline for Good Clinical Practice E6 (R1) (ICH-GCPs), and the EU Clinical Trials Directive, a freely given informed consent must be obtained from each participant for conducting a CT. The ICF is an important document and must be approved by the EC and overseen by the NRES. The ICF has to be provided to the MHRA along with the CTA.

The participant has to be provided all information relating to the study. The ICF should be easy to understand, brief and without coercion or unduly influencing the potential participant. As per the MHCTR, the ICF should be in English and all information along with it, whether oral or written, should also be in English. As per the MHCTR, the ICH-GCP, the participant and/or his/her legal representation and the investigator should sign and date the ICF. In case the participant is unable to read and is illiterate, verbal consent has to be obtained and an impartial witness has to be present who should countersign the form.

GERMANY

In Germany, a growing need for innovation to improve the quality and knowledge about CTs led to clinical research becoming a priority sector for the German government. This resulted in a new funding programme in the late 1990s by the Ministry of Education and Research under which new coordinating centres for CTs were established to strengthen academic clinical research in the country. The purpose of these centres has primarily been to support the development of new drugs and conduct trials within government affiliated German sites/hospitals. Some of these centres also provide advice to small pharmaceutical firms or academic investigators exploring drug development and are in the pre-clinical development phase for applications to competent authorities. Germany has been housing a large number of trials with its dense network of universities and faculty as well as a variety of research institutions and is the leader in industry-initiated clinical studies in Europe. However, it is reported that over time, the market for CTs in Germany has remained stagnant due to the reduced costs of conducting clinical research in other parts of the world with similar research infrastructure and quality of data.

The Regulatory Framework for Clinical Research

Overview of the Clinical Trial Review Process

A CTA review is done by the Federal Institute for Drugs and Medical Devices (BfArM) and Paul Ehrlich Institute (PEI) depending upon the type of the investigational medicinal product. After an initial administrative review of completeness of the application, the authority reviews the CTA through a formal and a contents team; both are done in parallel by separate units. The sponsor then gets one letter of conditional approval from the different teams. A name contact who is the sponsor's point of contact in the authority's office is provided.

The average time taken by ECs to review and approve trial protocols vary across provinces. At the moment, the formal timeline is 30 days for single site trials and 60 days for multi-site trials. The extended timeline for multi-site trials is due to the given time costs associated with contacting each institution's EC individually.

Ethics Committee Approval

The review of the CTA is done locally by the ECs, an arrangement that is distinct from other countries in the EU. The ECs in Germany are under three heads—Faculties of Medicine and Universities; Provincial Medical Associations and the ones directly attached to a province. The EC of the coordinating investigator becomes the coordinating EC and is responsible for the assessment of the project. It works in cooperation with all ECs who assess qualification of local sites and investigators. The local ECs may also comment on the protocol, but the coordinating EC is exclusively responsible for the ultimate decision on scientific and ethical aspects, which has come to be known as 'the single opinion' system.

Observation

> Some stakeholders suggested that there are different ways in which ECs discuss and decide the applications, e.g. some are very strict. Therefore, how the ECs at the end deal with the application is different and it makes it difficult for the investigators to plan out how it will work when they bring a complete application to these ECs. Further, the exchange of information between the coordinating and concerned ECs is not very smooth. This leads to longer time than required.

Observation from India

> In India, local ECs have discretion in deciding the amendments that the protocol needs to undertake in order to approve it at their site and in the absence of a 'one opinion' system, a multisite trial usually faces extended timelines for approval. However, involvement of local ECs allows for the close review of the suitability of the sites which is otherwise difficult.

Insurance and Indemnity Clauses

The insurance is done by the sponsor in addition to the health insurance of the participant. The amount of the insurance depends only on the risk of the procedure and the patient is informed ex ante about the amount and the degree of risk involved. However claim to insurance can only be made in cases where it can be demonstrated that the harm was related to the CT.

Observation

> In the experience of the several CT investigators, due to the adoption of a risk based approach, Serious Adverse Events (SAEs) leading to irreparable harm or death are very rare. No investigator witnessed an incident wherein the insurance amount has been paid to the trial participant.
>
> In both UK and Germany, several stakeholders reported the futility of taking insurance covers, which are rarely claimed due to widespread universal health coverage, but nevertheless followed the norm of taking the insurance cover.

Compensation for Participation; Injury and Death

In Germany, insurance cover for CTs is mandatory. Incidences involving compensations for harm related to a CT are rare. There is risk-adapted coverage. According to Section 40 (3) Arzneimittelgesetz (AMG- German Drug Law) in pharmaceutical drug trials: for each case of death or permanent disability at least €500,000 per person is provided for, irrespective of fault/blame or what is commonly referred to as verschuldensunabhängig (strict liability). The applicant/sponsor has to submit the confirmation of the insurer or a copy of the insurance policy:

- The policy must show that the individual trial is covered,
- The beginning and the end of the insurance period fits the planned trial schedule,
- The maximum insurance sum per person for each case of death or permanent disability is at least €500,000 per person,
- The insurance coverage applies regardless of fault/blame ("verschuldensunabhängig"),
- The general and specific conditions of the insurance contract are met.

Observation from India

> In India, usually a blanket insurance cover is taken by clinical institutions instead of an individual trial cover. This is very common for investigator initiated trials where there is no commercial entity acting as the sponsor. An analysis of the adequacy of such blanket covers is rarely possible.

Ethical Norms in Clinical Research

Informed Consent Process

The informed consent process used in Germany virtually mirrors that of the UK, except for the language requirements.

Observation

> The ICF in Germany was reported to be the most detailed. For instance, the contact details of the insurer are also provided in the form.

SINGAPORE

The Regulatory Framework for Clinical Research

Overview of the Clinical Trial Review Process

The Health Sciences Authority (HSA) is the NDRA in Singapore. The regulatory framework in Singapore governing CTs has undergone significant changes in the recent past with the aim to streamline the regulatory processes for pharmaceutical products. With effect from 15 July 2016, pharmaceutical products are now categorised as 'therapeutic products' and hence regulated under the Health Products Act and its subsidiary legislation, the Health Products (Clinical Trials) Regulations and require either Clinical Trial Authorisation or acceptance of Clinical Trial Notification (CTN) prior to initiation of the CT. Whereas CTs on cell lines, tissue and gene therapy products and complementary health products are still being regulated under the Medicines Act and its subsidiary legislation, the Medicines (Clinical Trials) Regulations and hence require a CTC to be granted prior to initiation of the clinical trial.

The clinical trials branch of the HSA has regulatory supervision of CTs on both therapeutic and medicinal products (e.g. pharmaceutical products, cell, tissue and gene therapy products, complementary health products) conducted in Singapore. A clinical study includes studies of phase 1 to 3 and BA/BE studies and the HSA reviews every CT application submitted to it by the sponsor. This review process is conducted parallel to the EC/IRB review process and it is the responsibility of the HSA to monitor clinical trial safety and conduct of GCP inspections. There is no requirement for the CT approval process in case of observational studies.

Ethics Committee Approval

The HSA used to follow the Singapore Guidelines for Good Clinical Practice (SG-GCP) which was adopted from the ICH GCP in 1998. However, as per the new regulatory changes, the SGGCP has been replaced by the ICH GCP E6 guidelines with effect from 1 November 2016. The ethics approval is to be obtained parallel to the HSA approval and the former is given by an IRB. The Ministry of Health (MoH) has also issued certain Ethical Guidelines on Research Involving Human Subjects [National Medical Ethical Committee(NMEC) Guidelines].[34] These guidelines issued by the are applicable to all research protocols involving human experimentation and all the hospitals are required to comply with these guidelines. All proposals are required to undergo an independent ethics review process and to comply with the ICH GCP guideline.

This is sent for approval first at the institutional level by the institution's EC or IRB, after getting approval, it is submitted to the HSA. The HSA then issues clinical trial certificate if the proposal is approved.

As per the new amendment which has come into effect from 1 November 2016, the existing CTC system will be expanded to include the CTA and CTN system. The new system now is risk based. Therefore, now if authorisation of CT by the HSA (for CTA) is required, then the IRB approval process can be made concurrently with the regulatory approval; if on the other hand in case of acceptance of a notification of CT by the HSA (for CTN) is required, the CTN application has to be submitted to HSA after receipt of the IRB approval letter.

Insurance and Indemnity Clauses

As per the Medical (Clinical Trials) Regulation, a CTC may be issued by the licensing authority subject to certain conditions. The licensing authority may impose a condition requiring the sponsor to obtain and maintain insurance to provide compensation in the event of injury or loss arising from the conduct of the CT. SG-GCP states that it is the duty of the sponsor to provide insurance to subjects. The ICH GCP state that if required by the regulatory requirements, the sponsor should provide insurance.

The Ministry of Health, Singapore, on their part came out with the national CT Insurance Policy in 2015 to harmonise the policy terms and coverage across all public healthcare institutions. Thus, all trials, studies, surveys and research conducted in Singapore by public healthcare institutions with ethics approval will be declared for insurance under the national CT insurance. 'Adequate' insurance cover is also a prerequisite for IRB approval. The MoH-National Medical Ethics' Committee recommendation update requires that institutions that allow non-physician investigators to do clinical studies should take out specific insurance cover for liabilities that these investigators may incur.

---

34. See, https://www.moh.gov.sg/content/dam/moh_web/Publications/Guidelines/National%20Medical%20Ethics%20Committee%20Guidelines/1997/human_bmr.pdf (Last accessed on 4 April 2017).

Compensation for Participation; Injury and Death

The standard practice is to use the ABPI Compensation Guidelines; however acceptability of the same varies across institutional settings. SG-GCP and the ICH-GCP state that a sponsor should be responsible for the compensation to the participants.

Since the SG-GCP was not clear on compensation guidelines and the MoH noticed an increase in phase 1 CTs, the MOH- National Medical Ethics' Committee came out with an update concerning phase 1 of CTs. The guidelines state the following:

- Sponsors of phase I trials, commercial or non-commercial, should make adequate and separate provisions for medical costs, and for compensation for non-medical costs for injuries sustained as a result of the clinical intervention or procedures provided for by the research protocol.

- Institutions that allow non-physician investigators to do clinical studies should take out specific insurance cover for liabilities that these investigators may incur.

- RECs should ensure that there are no gaps in responsibilities for providing for compensation for relevant non-medical costs and medical bills that arise from adverse events, and that responsibilities are spelt out clearly in the protocol and information sheet.

Medical costs and relevant compensation should be awarded on a no-fault basis.

The NMEC recommendations state that payments for participation in trials should be commensurate with the burden of participation.

Ethical Norms in Clinical Research

Informed Consent Process

Before a study is conducted, it is mandatory to obtain an ICF the participant. During this process, the investigators provide information to the subject about the research study. It is imperative that the subject has been adequately informed about the study, understood the risks and benefits involved and the subject should have voluntarily agreed to participate in the study. Everything about the study should be disclosed to the subject by the investigator. Once the subject is satisfied, he/she can choose to sign the consent form. In Singapore, informed consent is regulated by the Medicines (Clinical Trial) Regulations, ICH-GCP, SG-GCP and Guideline for Informed Consent in Unconscious or Mentally Incompetent Subjects.

As per the HSA, the basic elements of informed consent are information, comprehension and voluntariness, in accordance with the Belmont Report. Consent must be written, signed and dated by the subject.

The ICH-GCP and the SG-GCP categorically state that the ICF should be revised if some additional information becomes available and if this information is relevant to a subject's consent. This revised form should first be approved by the ECs. Informed consent is generally in English, and can be translated into local languages. The onus is on the sponsor to ensure that the translations are accurate. If the patient is literate in the local language, then an impartial witness may also act as translator. Both the subject and his/her legal representative should receive a copy of the signed written consent. After the commencement of the trial, in case there are any updates in the form, a copy of the updated and amended form should be given to the participant or his legal representatives.

INDONESIA

The Regulatory Framework for Clinical Research

Overview of the Clinical Trial Review Process

The National Agency of Drug and Food Control (NADFC) is the NDRA of Indonesia. It has a National Committee on Drug Evaluation (NCDE) comprising of experts in clinical pharmacology, pharmacy, qualified CT experts from various universities and institutes. Health research and R&D in healthcare are covered under the Indonesian Health Act No 23/1992. Besides this, CTs are also regulated under Decree of Head of NADFC 02002/SK/KBPOM, 2001 on 'Clinical Trial Procedure'.

In the year 2000, a clinical trial working group (CTWG) was established to improve the quality of CTs in Indonesia. In 2001, Indonesia implemented the Indonesia-GCP fully based on the ICH-GCP. All pre-market trials have to compulsorily follow the Indonesia GCP and they require approval from the NADFC before the trials can be initiated. The Scientific Committee/EC approvals are followed by regulatory approval from NADFC. Other than this, in case a company wants to ship biological samples for testing to get a globally harmonised result, it needs to obtain a material transfer agreement (MTA). The MTA is governed by the National Institute of Health Research and Development (NIHRD) of Indonesia.

Observation

> The minimum turnaround time for a CTA for a Phase 3 (from NADFCs end) was reported to be >12 weeks and above and varies depending upon the protocol, therapeutic category and other factors. Although there are defined timelines for the review in NADFC's mandate, the above figure is arrived at by factoring in the dead time in the review clock.

Ethics Committee Approval

The first EC in Indonesia was established in the year 1982. In Indonesia, the EC approval is necessary before the CTA can be submitted. ECs exist in most hospitals and institutions that conduct CTs. ECs in Indonesia follow the Indonesian-GCP guidelines. In 2002 by a Decree of Ministry of Health, a National Commission of Ethics in Health Research was established. It consists of 20 members including physicians, public health experts, lawyers, sociologists, pharmacists etc.

As per the Decree regarding CT procedure issued by the Ministry of Health, the institutions that conduct CTs need to have scientific committee and ECs. The scientific committee has to review the scientific aspect before approaching the EC. In case of absence of a scientific committee, the scientific aspects should be reviewed by the EC.

Insurance and Indemnity Clauses

As per the Indonesian-GCP, the sponsor must provide insurance to subjects and indemnify the investigator/institution against the claims arising from the trial.

Compensation for Participation; Injury and Death

The Indonesian GCP states that the sponsor should indemnify i.e. provide legal and financial coverage to the investigator/institution against claims arising from the trial except for claims that arise from malpractice or negligence. The sponsor's policies and procedures should address the costs of treatment of trial subjects in the event of trial related injury.

Observation

> Several stakeholders cited the ABPI guidelines on the subject matter as the most comprehensive and straight forward in interpretation.

Ethical Norms in Clinical Research

Informed Consent Process

A freely given, informed written consent is required to be obtained from each participant to comply with the requirements laid down in the GCP. The ICF and patient information sheet are viewed as essential documents that must be reviewed and approved by the EC and supplied to the licensing authority NADFC prior to beginning a CT.

Participant information should be presented in both written and oral form, whenever possible, and in nontechnical and understandable terms. When written consent as a signature or thumb impression is not possible, verbal consent may be taken after ensuring its documentation by an impartial witness.

Prior to participation in the trial, the subject or the subject's legal representative should receive a copy of the signed and dated written ICF and any other written information provided to the subjects.

4

**Under Trial:
The Challenge of
Clinical Trials in India**

Regulatory decision making is a legal procedure, based on scientific findings. In a capacity constrained milieu, regulatory decision making often turn into a mere procedure based on legal findings. The primary calculus behind regulatory decision making hence becomes anything but the pharmaceutical science of it. The case of rise and fall of CTs in India is a sordid tale of this sort of decision making. Drug regulation has an anomalous position in the Indian legal system. It has features of both the legislative and judicial processes but exists within a fragmented jurisdictional structure divided between the union and the states. Rules issued by the regulatory agency have a force that is equivalent to that of statutes, but they are not enacted by legislators. Adjudications by regulators have an effect that is similar to that of court rulings, but they are not conducted by judges. Finally by virtue of having a shared jurisdictional structure, differences in interpretation of the promulgated rules and the adjudications among the regulators located both at the union level as well as the state level, is a confounding factor for regulatory decision making. To top it off, the Indian drug regulation system shares most, if not all, of the maladies that afflict drug regulatory agencies in the developing world.

At the behest of the Hon'ble Supreme Court of India,[1] the regulatory landscape for clinical research in India witnessed an overhaul in the early 2013. In the aftermath of the changes, a flurry of mainstream media articles wrongly referred the aforementioned order as a ban on clinical research in India, while it is true that the number of ongoing and upcoming trials dipped from that point onwards, this was more to do with the wait and watch policy of sponsors[2] of CTs citing the supposedly stricter requirements to conduct CTs that were put forth. The foremost was that of providing for examination of SAEs and procedures for payment of compensation in case of CT related injury or death; the second was the audio-visual recording of the informed consent process; the third was the arbitrary cap on the number of trials an investigator could simultaneously undertake; the fourth was the requirement of a minimum threshold of public medical institutions (with predefined standards) to be chosen as CT sites[3] for multi-centric trials; the fifth was about inspection and monitoring of CTs and finally about registration requirements for ECs.

Most of these reforms although deeply desired, were rendered counterproductive in the absence of adequate regulatory guidance on specific issues, clarity on legal terminologies and a sound communication strategy. To add to the woes, the lack of an open resource[4] enumerating the nature of clinical trials conducted in India, led the public debate to take an undesirable turn. As a result, the global perception of India in the context of clinical research suffered a serious setback. The very changes put forth to rectify the regulatory system served as yet another source of confusion and uncertainty.

The case for paying compensation for an injury or death related to a CT is an excellent case at hand and the associated issues like that of use of standard of care, use of placebos, informed consent, etc. will be illustrated in the following subsections.

Compensation for trial related injury or death is a right of trial participant. The demand for compensation for injuries/death associated with clinical research is not new and several countries have provided for several national regulations and guidance so as to how these should be disbursed. For instance, Germany has some of the strictest rules for compensations of such nature. In almost all regulatory jurisdictions, developed or developing there is also a mandatory requirement to take an insurance cover in order indemnify those

---

1. The Hon'ble Supreme Court of India, vide its order dated 03.01.2013 in the matter of W.P. (C) No. 33/2012 of Swasthya Adhikar Manch, Indore & Anr Vs. Ministry of Health and Family Welfare & Ors. with WP(C) No. 779/2012 regarding CTs, had directed that until further orders by this Court, CTs of new chemical entity shall be conducted strictly in accord with the procedures prescribed in Schedule Y of the Drugs and Cosmetics Act, 1940 under the direct supervision of the Secretary, Ministry of Health and Family Welfare, Government of India.

2. Another reason cited behind the drop in clinical trials was the mandatory requirement of registration of ethics committees (ECs). As a matter of regulation, ECs across the globe have to be registered by a nodal agency. In India however, there was no such provision. Hence, registration of ECs was a welcome step. However, mere registration of an EC does not ensure compliance with Good Clinical Practices (GCP). The latter is ensured with periodic GCP inspections/audit of an EC, while accreditation by a recognized body helps this cause, but is a step yet to be implemented in India.

3. The third and the fourth requirement were taken off with the August 2016 CDSCO order, removing the restriction on the number of CTs an investigator can conduct at any time. See, http://www.cdsco.nic.in/writereaddata/restricion%20of%20conducting%20three.pdf; Further, the CDSCO order changed the requirement that trials be conducted at sites with more than 50 hospital beds to simply requiring the ethics committee to decide whether the site is suitable. See, http://www.cdsco.nic.in/writereaddata/requirement%20of%2050%20bedded%20.pdf.

4. Before a volunteer is recruited in a clinical study in India, it has to be registered with the Clinical Trial Registry of India (CTRI) which is an open repository for public use. However, the current structure of the database poses difficulties in undertaking a meta-analysis.

conducting a trial. This is not to be confused with medical malpractice insurance[5] often taken by the investigators conducting the trial, although, in the run up to the debate on clinical research, much differentiation has not been made between the two.

Out of the six jurisdictions that were visited, it was found that wherever possible the sponsor of the trial usually covers for the injury/death associated with the trial for a medicinal product. Most jurisdictions by virtue of being former British colonies follow the ABPI guidelines, which not only define when to provide for compensation but also limits the liability by expressly mentioning when not to provide for such compensation. The latter has been missing from the Indian rules, which has been the cause of much confusion and loss of positive perception.

Besides, the connotation associated with the term compensation in other jurisdictions is that of a payment for immediate harm. However, in the Indian rules, compensation is to be paid in case of an injury or death discerned at a later stage.[6] In the absence of specific guidance on specific therapeutic areas, this translates into a limitless liability for the sponsors of CTs. When the rule 122DAB was first inserted, the use of language such as, 'providing free medical management to CT as long as required in case of any injury irrespective of whether the injury is related to CT or not; providing financial compensation in case of injury or death due to failure of investigational product to provide intended therapeutic effect, and, use of placebo in placebo controlled trial', only add to the uncertainty.[7]

Thirdly, compensation in the Indian setting is tied to an analysis for 'relatedness', where the relatedness needs to be proven with the investigational product, which not only includes the drug under study but also the comparator arm—either an 'active control/standard of care' or an 'inactive control/placebo'.

This definition is akin to that in parlance in the EU where an investigational medicinal product also includes both the test and the comparator arms (see Table 4.1). But for the purpose of paying compensation, the term used in the ABPI guidelines is that of a 'medicinal product'. This subtle difference translates into dropping compensation for the comparator arm. Further, the ABPI guidelines categorically mention that in case of harm/injury/death associated with the standard of care, which would have been administered/prescribed to the patient/participant in the normal course of clinical practice, would not attract a compensation from the sponsor of the trial. The Indian rules, here were reported to function on the ethical principle of reciprocity, where by participating in a trial, a participant may be compensated for a trial related injury even when it arises by the use of a reference product in the comparator arm, although this has not been expressly mentioned in the rules.[8] The need for guidance is felt in this regard.

Table 4.1
Table Depicting Criteria for Compensation for Trial Related Injury/Death

Criteria for compensation for injury or death			
Causality to		Relatedness/Associated to	
Drug	Investigational Medicinal Product (IMP)	Drug	Investigational Product (IP)
USA	Singapore	Singapore	India
	EU	EU	
	Singapore	Singapore	
	Indonesia	Indonesia	
	South Africa	South Africa	
	India	USA	

Another issue for which guidance is required is, decoding the randomisation sequence in a double blinded global CT for imparting compensation. Cases were reported where the sponsor was not ready to disclose to which arm the participant was randomised to in order for compensation to be ascertained.

4.1 Use of Formulae for Calculating Compensation for Trial Related Injury/Death

Clinical research or the trial itself is not a commodity, but the resultant data is. Hence, in lieu of the commodity that a sponsor acquires, a participant or the investigator on behalf of the participant or the regulator from a public health perspective can

---

5. Medical professional liability insurance, sometimes known as medical malpractice insurance, is a type of professional liability insurance which protects physicians and other licensed health care professionals from liability associated with wrongful practices resulting in bodily injury, medical expenses and property damage, as well as the cost of defending lawsuits related to such claims.

6. See for instance, heading 4 under agenda no. 1, minutes of the 68th meeting of Drugs Technical Advisory Board (DTAB), held on 16th February, 2015. Available at: http://www.cdsco.nic.in/writereaddata/newMinutes%20of%2068th%20DTAB%20meeting.pdf (Last accessed on 4 April 2017).

7. See, section 3.2 for the amended Rule 122DAB, where all the above statements have been amended by adding a qualifier.

8. However, this is expressly mentioned in the Prof Ranjit Roy Committee report.

mandate a sponsor to pay compensations for trial related/associated death/injury. However, with formulae to compute the quantum of liability under different set of conditions/scenarios (based on risk/age/disease profile), the mandate virtually transforms a 'social norm' into an 'economic norm'.

This is reportedly an unprecedented move in the domain of clinical research where the normative contract between the participant and the sponsor alters into an economic pact which can have an 'endowment effect'[9] in the future.

However, most stakeholders interviewed were found to be in support of the formulae. Save for one instance, quoted in Case Study 4, every stakeholder from the industry interviewed shared that the formulae bring a cap on the liability and the quantum calculated comes out to be fair. Most academicians were either of the view that these formulae compute a fair quantum for compensation and that it is too soon to assess their impact on clinical research.

Observation

> The formulae although unique for the domain of clinical research, have found currency among several stakeholders interviewed. Industry hails the formulae primarily because it practically puts a cap on the liability borne by the sponsor.

4.2 Use of a 'Standard of Care'

The initial Rule 122DAB mandated compensation for *"use of placebo in a placebo-controlled trial"*, however the clause was later qualified and now reads, *"use of placebo in a placebo-controlled trial where, the standard of care, though available, was not provided to the participant as per trial protocol"*. In absence of a definition of and clear guidance on what constitutes a 'standard of care,'[10]

the impact of the alteration stands to be limited.

Several practitioners and investigators across the country informed that a non-universal local 'standard of care' is almost always provided in the control arm in a CT. A local standard of care in the Northern provinces of the country hence may not be same as that used in the Southern provinces. Interestingly, it was found that the Head of Departments (HODs) who in many instances are also key opinion leaders in the domain of clinical research, usually set a standard of care for an institution or a division. The peers and pupils then propagate it both as matter of routine clinical practice and in research. Hence, formulating a general recommendation that could be applied to all situations in this regard is not feasible.

4.3 Use of Placebos in a Placebo Controlled Trial

Rule 122DAB prescribes that placebo-controlled trials are justified when there is no other proven treatment. However, the use of a placebo remains controversial when an effective treatment does exist. It was in 2002, that the World Medical Association published a note of clarification[11] for 'Declaration of Helsinki' on the use of placebos stating that, where proven therapy is available, a placebo may be used only 'for compelling and scientifically sound methodological reasons' or when the risks to the participants are insignificant and the condition being studied is minor. Since then, this has been the 'dictum' for using placebos in human experimentation followed in most countries. As is the case with the use of a 'standard of care', formulating a general recommendation that could be applied to all situations in this regard is not feasible. Several stakeholders agreed that the use of placebos would have to be considered on a case by case basis.

4.4 Clinical Trial Waivers

A local clinical study requirement is based on the assumption that differences in ethnicity might lead to pharmacological differences which ultimately translates to varied efficacy of the intervention in

---

9. In psychology and behavioural economics, the endowment effect (also known as divestiture aversion and related to the mere ownership effect in social psychology) is the hypothesis that people ascribe more value to things merely because they own them. This has happened in the health insurance sector and jurisdictions with universal health coverage. Several studies from behavioural economics have shown that once an endowment if effected, any attempt of reversal to an earlier state is rarely possible. Formulae for compensation for injury or death (related to a trial) can effect such an endowment.

10. A standard of care may be universal or non-universal. The term 'universal standard of care' is usually defined as the best current treatment available anywhere in the world; the term 'non-universal standard of care' refers to regional and local standards that might entail a lower level of care. The costs of providing a particular standard of care may not be confined merely to the cost of providing medicines, but

may also include the related costs of improvements to the healthcare system and infrastructure. A requirement for a universal standard could prevent research that has the potential to benefit people in developing countries from being undertaken. For example, research which aimed to compare a new treatment with one currently available to the target population might not be possible (see, NCOB 2002).

11. See, note of clarification on paragraph 29 of the WMA Declaration of Helsinki, available at: http://biotech.law.lsu.edu/cases/research/helsinki.htm (Last accessed on 4 April 2017).

> **Case Study 3**
>
> **From Causality to Relatedness: Compensating SAEs in Clinical Research**
>
> One of the issues faced by the clinical research community globally is assessment of the causal association of adverse events to investigational products. While numerous methods for causality assessment of adverse events have been published in the past, few have focused on the issue exclusively from a clinical trials perspective. The WHO-UMC system of causality assessment was designed primarily for pharmacovigilance as a tool to use in the assessment of case reports. While the WHO-UMC system provides a structure that can be applied to adverse events in clinical trials, it was not designed specifically for use with investigational agents before approval and labelling; the drug label includes a summary of the essential information needed for the safe and effective use of the drug, including both common and serious adverse events are detailed.
>
> The ISCR (Indian Society for Clinical Research) and the MRCT (Muli-Regional Clinical Centre), Harvard recognised a need to develop a more specific tool which will help standardize causality assessment in the setting of clinical trials. The tools expands upon the existing WHO-UMC system and represents a comprehensive framework for clinical trials case causality assessment. The framework lists 22 items of information and provides an assessment questionnaire (alogrithm) with 29 binary-response questions. The responses to the individual questions in the questionnaire can be plotted against essential and supplementary criteria for classification of an event into one of the 4 WHO-UMC causality categories: 'certain', 'probable', 'possible' and 'unlikely'.
>
> The framework is an algorithm-based non-proprietary tool that has the potential to enhance standardisation of case causality assessment in clinical trials and allow greater reliance on the use of the WHO-UMC system in clinical research.
>
> The causality assessment can then be used to arrive at a decision on whether an SAE was related or unrelated to a clinical trial.

> **Case Study 4**
>
> **A Paediatric Vaccine Trial**
>
> A renowned vaccine R&D firm shifted a major vaccine trial from India to a neighbouring country, primarily because of two reasons. The first was a purely scientific reason—the epidemiology of the disease was well charted out in the country to which it was sourced, while this was not true to that extent for India. The second was for the commercial reason of containing costs being incurred for complying with insurance norms to conduct clinical trials in India.
>
> In order to provide an insurance cover for compensations arising from any injury or death related to a trial, the firm had to shell out a hundred fold premium as compared to what was being charged by the insurance company in the country where is was ultimately sourced to.
>
> The reason for the high premium was cited to be the existing rate of child mortality and the compensation formula for trial-related death where compensation for a trial participant below the age of 17 goes over ₹ 70 lakh (over USD 100,000). In order to indemnify the sponsor of the liability arising out of this requirement, the premium quoted was a hundred fold vis-à-vis the prevailing premia in the neighbouring country.

different populations. Literature on both supporting as well as rejecting the assumption exists, without a conclusive answer because lack of resources has resulted in the lack of significant data.[12]

The eventual aim to conduct a CT is to introduce a new drug to a population which also contributes as trial participants. On the other hand, the eventual aim of a post marketing study and long term pharmacovigilance is to remove a drug from a population based on its long term impact. While the former is to establish efficacy in a clinical setting, the latter is about establishing the effectiveness in a non-clinical setting. In the absence of a robust long

---

12. From a purist pharmacological perspective though, only those drugs which affect the first pass metabolism can manifest varied pharmacological profiles. This, however is, beginning to change with personalised medicine based on pharmacogenomics.

term pharmacovigilance mechanism in India the onus of proving long term 'safety' is pushed as the requirement of conducting a local bridging study.

Several stakeholders questioned the scientific basis of conducting a local CT with two hundred odd patients. Most investigators interviewed were of the opinion that such trials serve no purpose, but to fulfil a legal requirement.

Observation

> The rationale for instituting local bridging trials assumes that most clinical end points can be verified with a given number of participants from an ethnic group. Irrespective of the CT design, the sample size for a majority of bridging trials in India varies between 100-200 trial participants.

4.5 Mandatory Local Filing of Marketing Authorisation After the Clinical Trial

In 2013 it was mooted that at the time of any global CT application, a condition should be stipulated in the permission letter/NOC that as and when the chemical/molecular/biological entity is approved and launched in other country/countries, the sponsor/applicant shall be required to file application seeking marketing of the same drug in the Indian market.

Most stakeholders including those from the Industry were in support of this reform. Other countries like South Africa also have such an express requirement in a CT application. However it was informed that in the absence of an adequate follow up by the regulatory authority, such a clause is rendered ineffective.

4.6 Audio-visual Recording of Informed Consent

Audio/visual recording of an informed consent for a clinical study may be required under a few circumstances in fewer regulatory jurisdictions. However, a mandatory requirement for audio-visual recording of informed consent is unique to the Indian setting.[13] Most international responders dismayed at the mandatory requirement. Responses from the Indian stakeholders were mixed. Those in support cited that the requirement of an audio-visual recording of an informed consent helps mitigate therapeutic misunderstanding while concomitantly protects the investigator of any liability due to malpractice. Those against the requirement cited several uncertainties in the mandated guideline:

a) A broad connotation to the term 'vulnerable person/population' entails that anybody and everybody can stand to be 'vulnerable' under different contexts. The conundrum warrants a detailed guidance from the regulator.

b) Audio-visual recording may not be feasible for several clinical conditions. For instance, investigators undertaking therapeutic studies for psychological disorders expressed concerns with the requirement being mandatory. In several instances it was suggested that it is problematic to place a camera in front of a CT participant who is also patient of a psychological disorder. The modality for a legal representative should be explicitly defined under such instances.

c) Other concerns like that of trial participant's privacy rights; mode of media capture and storage, etc. were voiced.

Almost all stakeholders demanded for a detailed written guidance from the regulator on the issue of audio-visual recording.

4.7 Message Fidelity in Translated Informed Consent Forms

Several stakeholders commented that consent forms are often designed to ring fence those undertaking the trials, rather than participants. As a result, a lot of jargon is used in the Informed consent sheet, with a single translation-back-translation cycle'[14] from 'English to Vernacular' the original meaning tends to transmute. This practice persists as it is usually not possible to simplify the contents of the form from a legal standpoint.

The problem of maintaining message fidelity on back translation of content of the informed consent

---

13. Since 2015, this requirement was restricted for 'vulnerable participants' in trials of New Chemical Entities or New Molecular Entities. However except for a few examples, what constitutes 'vulnerable population' is not expressly defined in the D&C Rules. Other documents of authority also define the term with a broad connotation. See for instance, the existing ethics guidelines for conduct of biomedical research on human subjects by ICMR and the draft ethics guidelines, 2016.

14. For the purpose of recruiting participants from non-English speaking population pools, the informed consent forms are first translated in the local/native language of the population and then back-translated to English to ensure a faithful translation.

form was found to be one of the key problems in the informed consent process. Often the biomedical jargon is transliterated instead of being translated. This requires a domain specific machine aided translation solution that can mitigate therapeutic misunderstanding by translating in multiple Indian languages.

In the course of the fieldwork, several models where such a solution has been deployed were shown to add to the efficiency of the functioning of ECs. In India, under the stewardship of the Forum for Ethics Review Committees in India (FERCI), a project called 'CreateEthics' found to be pertinent. The IT solutions being developed under this project can go a long way in solving the problem of translating ICFs (refer to Case Study 1).

4.8 Trends in Clinical Research in Other Countries

a. Increased regulatory reliance on ECs

Scientific review of CTAs consumes significant regulatory bandwidth. It is an increasing trend world over to delegate as much clinical review workload (as is permissible from the perspective of risk involved) to ECs. An example at the extreme is that of the Australian Therapeutic Goods Administration (TGA), which has employed a laissez faire approach towards CT application review (across all phases). It has employed an across the board Clinical Trial Notification System, relieving TGA of significant regulatory bandwidth to be deployed elsewhere. The notifications system is often cited to be the reason that has made Australia one of the preferred destinations for conducting CTs.[15] A similar but not so radical example is that of Singapore, where a notification system for trials with minimal risk has only been instituted from November 2016. In all these cases there has been an increasing delegation of duties to the ECs for a scientific review.

Observation

> The CDSCO Notice in March 2016 for completely relying on ECs for review of academic trials was reported to be a key move that would free up significant regulatory bandwidth for CDSCO to focus on regulatory trials.

b. Central vs Local Ethical Review: Single IRB for multi-site research

The EC requirements for clinical research were instituted in an era when most CTs were conducted at a single study site or at a small number of sites. There has been tremendous growth in clinical research activity since then and there has been increasing use of multi-site/regional CTs to better manage overall trials. In the era of mega trials the use of a centralised ethical review where the local ethical committees fully or partly rely on the review of an offsite ethics committee is beginning to take hold. On 21 June 2016, the National Institutes of Health, USA, issued a policy on the "Use of a Single Institutional Review Board for Multi-Site Research" *"to enhance and streamline the IRB review process in the context of multi-site research so that research can proceed as effectively and expeditiously as possible"*. It is stated that eliminating duplicative IRB review is expected to reduce unnecessary administrative burdens and systemic inefficiencies without diminishing protection for human subjects. The shift in workload away from conducting redundant reviews is also expected to allow IRBs to concentrate more in terms of time and attention on the review of single site protocols, thereby enhancing research oversight.

From 25 May 2017 onwards, all federally funded research in the US, would be based on a single IRB of record for the trial. All the participating institutions will have to rely on the review of the single IRB of record. Similarly, in Australia a National Mutual Recognition System for IRBs has been put in place, where again a single IRB of record reviews a clinical trial application while the other review boards rely on this review, rendering the process more effective.

With the rise of global clinical programmes and hence multi-country, multi-site CTs, several countries have instituted mechanisms to allow an EC to rely on scientific and ethics review of another EC, while taking the responsibility of local oversight. However, the Indian regulations have followed a counter-trend. Earlier, under the Schedule Y to D&C Rules, trial site(s) were allowed to accept the approvals granted to a protocol by the ethics committee of another trial site or an approval granted by an independent ethics committee (constituted as per Appendix VIII of the schedule), provided that the approving ethics committee(s) willingly accepted their responsibilities for the study at such trial site(s) and the trial site(s) willingly accepted such an arrangement given the protocol version is same at all trial sites. This

---

15. See, "Australia: Preferred Destination for Early Phase Clinical Trials", White Paper, Frost and Sullivan 2016.

however has been discontinued[16] and independent ECs are now restricted to review only BA/BE protocols.

c. Post-Trial Access to Investigational Product

The 2013 iteration of the Declaration of Helsinki states that "*In advance of a clinical trial, sponsors, researchers and host country governments should make provisions for post-trial access for all participants who still need an intervention identified as beneficial in the trial. This information must also be disclosed to participants during the informed consent process.*" A national guidance by the MCC on Post Trial Access to investigational product was floated for public comment in June 2013. The language in the guidance borrows the terminology of "benefit"[17] from the 2013 iteration of Declaration of Helsinki. The use of this term was reported to be too broad by many stakeholders in the industry. It was argued that for chronic conditions that last a life time, post-trial access in the absence of a clearly defined timeline may mean a lifetime responsibility of making a medicine available to a subject.

The problem was reported all the more acute in countries with inadequate health coverage, leading to significant out of pocket expenditures on drugs. Post-trial access is increasingly becoming a subject of key concern as several countries are beginning to host global clinical studies.

Regulatory authorities in India have taken note and recommendation of the Drugs Technical Advisory Board (DTAB) are key in this regard.[18] DTAB recommended that "*Post Trial access of the investigational products may be provided to the clinical trial participant, if during the course of the trial, an investigational product is found to be beneficial. This is to be based on the recommendations of the investigator and ethics committee, especially in cases where no alternative therapy is available to the patient. However, such Post Trial access of the investigational product should be permitted after obtaining the consent of the patient, however, there would not be any liability of the sponsor in use of the drug. The sponsor shall arrange to provide the drug in such cases free of cost as the drug might not yet have been permitted to be marketed. Drugs and Cosmetics Rules, 1945 may be amended appropriately.*"

4.9 Policy Recommendations

Challenge 1: Empowering Ethics Committees

> **Recommendation 1:** NABH and FERCI should develop an IT enabled platform that enables ECs to manage a research project throughout its life cycle (refer to Case Study 1).

Rationale: IT enabled platforms for project management by ECs were found be extremely useful in several countries.

Target Agency: NABH; FERCI; NIC.

> **Recommendation 2:** A web based interactive GCP learning module should be developed and online training using the module should be mandatory for every EC member.

Rationale: GCP Training delivered by online modules is a standard practice followed in USA, EU and several other countries. This helps members to stay updated.

Target Agency: NABH; CDSCO; ICMR.

> **Recommendation 3:** NABH should draft model Standard Operating Procedures (SOPs) for ECs.

Rationale: Model SOPs are reported to aid in uniform implementation of GCP.

Target Agency: NABH, CDSA, ICMR, FERCI.

> **Recommendation 4:** NABH should sign MoUs with other agencies of standing to aiding faster accreditation of ECs in India.

Rationale: Leveraging expertise in other accreditation bodies can help establish in-house expertise at NABH.

Target Agency: NABH; QCI.

---

16. See Agenda No. 4, in minutes of the 66th meeting of DTAB, held on 16 January 2014, CDSCO, New Delhi, Available at: http://www.cdsco.nic.in/writereaddata/Minutes%20of%20 66th%20DTAB%20meeting.pdf (Last accessed on 4 April 2017).

17. The term 'benefit' or 'beneficial' is a relative term as it is often difficult to quantify the benefit of an investigational product compared to the standard of care. The term was found to be of much debate in South Africa where a guidance document had been drafted on "POST CLINICAL TRIAL DRUG ACCESS" by the Medicines Control Council, South Africa. Available at: http://www.mccza.com/documents/ f27b533e2.42_Post_Clinical_Trial_Drug_Access_Apr16_v1.pdf (Last accessed on 4 April 2017).

18. See Agenda No. 1, bullet 3 in minutes of the 68th meeting of DTAB, held on 16th February, 2015, CDSCO, New Delhi, Available at: http://www.cdsco.nic.in/writereaddata/ newMinutes%20of%2068th%20DTAB%20meeting.pdf (Last accessed on 4 April 2017).

Challenge 2: Making consent more informed

Recommendation 5: Development of IT enabled tools for a more meaningful translation of Informed Consent Forms (ICF) into vernacular languages (refer to Case Study 1).

Rationale: The current mechanism of translating and back translating ICF into vernacular are often motivated to ring-fence and protect those undertaking clinical research rather than those participating in such research.

Target Agency: NABH; FERCI; ICMR; CDAC.

Recommendation 6: Development of audio-visual aids for deployment before consent for clinical research (refer to Case Study 2).

Rationale: It is difficult to simplify the contents of the ICF for legal reasons. Deployment of audio-visual aids have been found to facilitate the CT participants in making more informed choices in low-resource settings.

Target Agencies: ISCR; OPPI, IPA, IDMA; Sponsors; ICMR.

Recommendation 7: Development of a final technical guidance on audio-visual recording of informed consent process in CTs.

Rationale: Audio-visual recording of informed consent process is not feasible for several disease conditions.[19]

Target Agencies: CDSCO.

Challenge 3: Compensating for injury or death related to a clinical trial

Recommendation 8: In addition to global introspection methodology, adoption of an algorithm for causality assessments to helping arriving at a decision on relatedness of an injury/death to an investigational product (refer to Case Study 1).

Rationale: Objective algorithms are shown to bring uniformity in causality assessments and helps in building a broad consensus on final assessments.

Target Agencies: CDSCO, ISCR.

Recommendation 9: CDSCO should adopt a more focused approach towards passing orders for compensation for injury or death related to a trial.[20] For cases where an EC agrees to compensate a CT participant and the sponsor agrees to pay adequate compensation, submitting an authenticated proof of payment along with the SAE report to the DCG(I) should complete the SAE reporting cycle.

Rationale: An analysis for relatedness (in case of injury or death) by an EC, recommending to provide compensation to a CT participant is unlikely to be overturned by the regulatory authority or the SAE expert committee.

Target Agencies: CDSCO.

Challenge 4: Addressing uncertainty

Recommendation 10: CDSCO should devise a comprehensive communication strategy for its policies, decisions and regulatory thinking on matters under their mandate.

Rationale: The often cited problem with CDSCO was the lack of a formal communication strategy. Stakeholders communicated difficulties in navigating the drug regulator's website, the lack of a notification system for updates on notices, orders etc. and the fact that things are often communicated verbally.

Target Agencies: CDSCO.

Recommendation 11: CDSCO should delegate an independent body to undertake regulatory impact assessment of the regulatory changes brought to the D&C Rules that affected CTs.

Rationale: Revision of technical guidance documents are based on assessments of past changes in the regulation.

Target Agencies: CDSCO.

---

19. Several experts and clinical investigators with experience of conducting clinical studies on patients with existing psychological disorders expressed concerns about taking consents from such subjects in front of cameras.

20. See Agenda S1 under minutes for 73rd DTAB meeting, available at: http://www.cdsco.nic.in/writereaddata/73_DTAB_Minutes%20as%20approved%20_.pdf (Last accessed on 3 April 2017).

> **Recommendation 12:** The already proposed provision of Pre-Submission Meetings[21] of CTs applicants with subject experts should be implemented.

Rationale: NDRAs across the world have pre-submission consultations as a regular feature with the aim to bring transparency, accountability, predictability and speedy regulatory approvals.

Target Agencies: CDSCO.

> **Recommendation 13:** In the long term, CDSCO should strive to build in-house capacity for scientific and ethic review of CT protocols.

Rationale: Across the globe, having in-house expertise within National Drug Regulatory Authorities aids speedy disposal of applications.

Target Agencies: CDSCO.

Challenge 5: Miscellaneous Issues

> **Recommendation 14:** The newly drafted D&C Rules for CTs should include a provision for PTA to beneficial investigational products and a detailed technical guidance should be formulated. DTAB recommendations in this regard should be implemented.

Rationale: An investigational drug is unlikely to be generally available to the community or population until sometime after the conclusion of the study/trial. Provisions for Post-Trial Access is a key issue being currently addressed worldwide.

Target Agencies: CDSCO.

Recommendation 15: CDSCO should draft a detailed guidance on what constitutes a 'standard of care' [22] for use in clinical studies.

Rationale: In the absence of a regulatory definition of 'standard of care', a general advice on using a standard of care cannot be applied to all situations.

Target Agencies: CDSCO.

> **Recommendation 16:** Define conditions for a CT waiver and institute an accelerated approval pathway for drugs already approved in stricter regulatory jurisdictions.

Rationale: Clinical data from local bridging studies in India has not led to a single drug being denied marketing approval.[23]

Target Agencies: CDSCO.

> **Recommendation 17:** CTRI should restructure the database to improve public access to information.

Rationale: In-depth trend/meta-analysis of CT entries from the CTRI dataset is currently problematic.

Target Agencies: CTRI, NIMS, ICMR.

---

21. See Notice Dated: 28th January, 2015, available at: http://www.cdsco.nic.in/writereaddata/NOTICE15.pdf (Last accessed on 3 April 2017).
22. A standard of care may be universal or non-universal. The term 'universal standard of care' is usually defined as the best current treatment available anywhere in the world; the term 'non-universal standard of care' refers to regional and local standards that might entail a lower level of care. The costs of providing a particular standard of care may not be confined merely to the cost of providing medicines, but may also include the related costs of improvements to the healthcare system and infrastructure. A requirement for a universal standard can prevent research that has the potential to benefit people in developing countries from being undertaken. For example, research which aims to compare a new treatment with one currently available to the target population might not be possible. For a more detailed exposition see, report titled "The ethics of research related to healthcare in developing countries", Nuffield Council On Bioethics, 2002; available at: http://nuffieldbioethics.org/wp-content/uploads/2014/07/Ethics-of-research-related-to-healthcare-in-developing-countries-I.pdf (Last accessed on 4 April 2017).
23. Rule 122A in DCR, 1945, states, "Provided that the requirement of submitting the results of local clinical trials may not be necessary if the drug is of such a nature that the Licensing Authority may, in public interest decide to grant such permission on the basis of data available from other countries", and hence provides for the waiver of the requirement of local CTs in India. An idea was mooted during the term of the erstwhile DCG(I) that for applications with clinical data evaluated by certain predefined regulatory jurisdictions classified as 'strict', the requirement of local CT may be waived off, but this was never brought into practice. However a similar provision was brought via an office order in 2015 for biosimilars. See Appendix VI, entry 16a. This idea is again doing rounds in policy circles, see for instance, Agenda No. S-2, minutes of the 75th meeting of Drugs Technical Advisory Board (DTAB), held on 3 January 2017. Available at: http://www.cdsco.nic.in/writereaddata/Minutes%20of%2075th%20DTAB%20held%20on%2003_01_2017.pdf (Last accessed on 4 April 2017).

5

Conclusions

The Government of India needs to develop a supportive framework for conduct of clinical trials—now more than ever, sooner rather than later. From a public health perspective—which is of central concern for drug regulators—our overwhelming burden of disease, disability and premature deaths (the highest worldwide) is holding the nation and its citizens back from achieving their potential. We are in dire need of newer and better medicines, inter alia to address our health challenges. A nation that has all prerequisites to be a world leader in clinical research and development has been suffering massive public health and economic losses due to uncertainty surrounding the issue.

Early participation in global clinical research programmes is in the interest of the country, given these studies are relevant, scientific and ethically conducted. We need to develop consensus around these issues among various stakeholders and enhance regulatory capacity to address the mistrust that has plagued the perception and prospects of clinical research in the country. Pharmaceutical companies largely conduct clinical trials in countries where they prefer to launch their new medicines earlier rather than later. By being part of global clinical trials—which, contrary to general understanding, currently constitute a quantitatively insignificant yet qualitatively significant proportion of clinical trials conducted in India—we not only gain in terms of the science and economics invested in the conduct of clinical trials, we incentivise global drug discovery which is sensitive to our local public health requirements as well as earlier introduction of the newest medicines from around the world.

To achieve this, India needs to improve its global image on the issue of clinical trials. In interviews conducted in six countries across four continents, key stakeholders driving global clinical research communicated their inability to comprehend and follow Indian requirements due to lack of detailed guidance on several issues. Transparency and regular dialogue with all relevant stakeholders in the domain of clinical research is the first step to take things forward. According to WHO, NDRAs in maturing regulatory jurisdictions need not have completely new guidelines—the simplest approach is to adapt from existing ones which are in sync with both local and global contexts. Besides, WHO guidelines are available on most technical requirements for various categories of pharmaceuticals. Some NDRAs even choose to rely on decisions made by NDRAs in other countries, while others use scientific reports prepared by other NDRAs. The use of scientific reports prepared by experts in other national jurisdictions does not mean adopting them without discretion or any infringement or loss of sovereign rights, rather a healthy sharing of expert resources already available out there. Countries learn from each other to move ahead—they don't have to reinvent the wheel every time.

The Indian pharmaceutical industry has done well in the space of generics. It now needs to mature into drug discovery and innovation, a process which has already started among the leading players. Policymakers need to accelerate that process to address our public health needs and provide a boost to one of the key sectors of our economy. The Indian pharmaceutical industry requires a dynamic ecosystem rather than handholding patronage from policymakers in order to grow to the next level. A promotive ecosystem and clear set of policies and guidelines around clinical trials hold the key.

References

Angell, M. (1988). "Ethical imperialism?", *New England Journal of Medicine* 319(16): 1081-83.

Armitage, P. (2003). "Fisher, Bradford Hill, and randomization", *International Journal of Epidemiology*, 32(6): 925-28.

Barnes, M., M.C. Minal, A. Varghese and E.B. Bierer (2015). *India's Proposed Amendments to the Drug and Cosmetics Act: Compensation for Injuries to Clinical Trial Participants and the Criminalization of Clinical Research.* Life Sciences Law & Industry Report, 09 LSLR 117. USA: The Bureau of National Affairs, Inc.

Barry, M. (1988). "Ethical considerations of human investigation in developing countries", *New England Journal of Medicine* 319(16): 1083-86

DiMasi, J.A., R.W. Hansen and H.G. Grabowski (2003). "The price of innovation: new estimates of drug development costs", *Journal of health economics* 22(2): 151-85.

DiMasi, J.A., R.W. Hansen, H.G. Grabowski and L. Lasagna (1991). "Cost of innovation in the pharmaceutical industry", *Journal of health economics* 10(2): 107-42

Dorsey, E.R., J. de Roulet, J.P. Thompson, J.I. Reminick, A. Thai, Z. White-Stellato and H. Moses (2010). "Funding of US biomedical research, 2003-2008", *JAMA* 303(2): 137-43.

Emanuel, E.J., D. Wendler J. Killen and C. Grady (2004). "What makes clinical research in developing countries ethical? The benchmarks of ethical research", *Journal of Infectious Diseases* 189(5): 930-37.

Fried C., (1974). *Medical Experimentation: Personal Integrity and Social Policy.* New York: American Elsevier.

Garnier, J.P. (2008). "Rebuilding the R&D engine in big pharma", *Harvard business review* 86(5): 68-70.

Gautam, C.S. and L. Saha (2008). "Fixed dose drug combinations (FDCs): Rational or irrational—A view point", *British Journal of Clinical Pharmacology* 65(5): 795-96.

Glickman, S.W., J.G. McHutchison, E.D. Peterson, C.B. Cairns, R.A. Harrington, R.M. Califf and K.A. Schulman (2009). "Ethical and scientific implications of the globalization of clinical research", *New England Journal of Medicine* 360(8): 816-23.

Griffin, J.P. (Ed.) (2009). *The Textbook of Pharmaceutical Medicine.* John Wiley & Sons.

Gulhati, C.M. (2003). "Irrational fixed-dose drug combinations: A sordid story of profits before patients", *Issues Med Ethics* 11(5).

Hamowy, R. (2010). *Medical Disasters and the Growth of FDA: Policy Report.* Oakland CA, USA: The Independent Institute.

Herper, M. (2013). "The cost of creating a new drug now $5 billion, pushing big pharma to change", *Forbes* 8(11).

Horng, S. and C. Grady (2003). "Misunderstanding in clinical research: Distinguishing therapeutic misconception, therapeutic misestimation and therapeutic optimism", *IRB: Ethics & Human Research* 25(1): 11-16.

ICH Harmonised Tripartite Guideline (1996). *Guideline for Good Clinical Practice E6 (R1).* International Council on Harmonisation of Technical Requirements for Registration of Pharmaceuticals for Human Use. 10 June. https://www.ich.org/fileadmin/Public_Web_Site/ICH_Products/Guidelines/Efficacy/E6/E6_R1_Guideline.pdf

International Council on Harmonisation Steering Committee. (1998). "Guidance on ethnic factors in the acceptability of foreign clinical data", *Fed Regist* 63(111): 31790-96.

Limaye, D., J.M. Langer, T. Rühling and G. Fortwengel (2015). "A critical appraisal of clinical trials conducted and subsequent drug approvals in India and South Africa", *BMJ open* 5(8): e007304

Lorenzo, C., V. Garrafa, J.H. Solbakk and S. Vidal (2010). "Hidden risks associated with clinical trials in developing countries", *Journal of Medical Ethics* 36(2): 111–15.

Marshall, D.A. and M. Hux (2009). "Design and analysis issues for economic analysis alongside clinical trials", *Medical care* 47(7_Supplement_1): S14-S20.

Matthews, J. R. (1995). *Quantification and the Quest for Medical Certainty.* Princeton University Press

Mazzetti, P., G. Silva-Paredes and M. Cornejo-Olivas (2012). "Role of government in clinical trials", *Revista Peruana de Medicina Experimental y Salud Pública* 29(4): 509-15.

Mehdi, A., D. Chaudhry, P. Tomar and P. Joshi (2016). "Prevention of chronic diseases: Reorienting primary health systems in India", *ICRIER Working Paper* 321. New Delhi: Indian Council for Research on International Economic Relations.

Meinert, C.L. (2012). *Clinical Trials: Design, Conduct and Analysis.* Oxford University Press

Meyers, E. (2006). *Globalization of Drug Development: India.* Cambridge Healthtech Associates

Mondal, S. and D. Abrol (2015). Clinical Trials Industry in India: A Systematic Review, ISID Working Paper 179, Institute for Studies in Industrial Development.

Müller, L. and E. Husar (2013). *Preclinical safety testing. The Textbook of Pharmaceutical Medicine.* Edited by J.P. Griffin. 7th Edition. pp.42-81.

O'Brien, Bernie. (1996). "Economic evaluation of pharmaceuticals: Frankenstein's monster or vampire of Trials?", *Medical Care* 34(12): DS99-DS108.

Petryna, A. (2005). "Ethical variability: drug development and globalizing clinical trials", *American Ethnologist* 32(2): 183-97

Piantadosi, S. (2013). *Clinical Trials: A Methodologic perspective.* John Wiley & Sons

Pratt, B., D. Zion and B. Loff (2012). "Evaluating the capacity of theories of justice to serve as a justice framework for international clinical research", *The American Journal of Bioethics* 12(11): 30-41.

Randal, J. (1999). "Randomized controlled trials mark a golden anniversary", *Journal of the National Cancer Institute* 91(1): 10-12

Pollock, Allyson A. Patricia McGettigan, Peter Roderick, Roger Jeffery and Rushikesh Mahajan (2014). "Need for a new drugs bill", *Economic & Political Weekly* XLIX(33), 16 August.

Rodwin, M.A. and J.D. Abramson (2012). "Clinical trial data as a public good", *JAMA* 308(9): 871-72.

Shapiro, A.K. and E. Shapiro (2000). *The Powerful Placebo: From Ancient Priest to Modern Physician.* JHU Press

Smyth, R.L. and A.M. Weindling (1999) "Research in children: Ethical and scientific aspects", *The Lancet* 354 (Suppl 2): SII21-4, September.

Spilker, B. (1992). *Guide to Clinical Trial.* New York: Raven Press. p.1156.

Suzanne W. J. (2008). "FDA and Clinical Drug Trials: A Short History", in Madhu Davies and Faiz Kerimani (eds.), *A Quick Guide to Clinical Trials.* Washington: Bioplan, Inc. pp.25-55

Thatte, U.M. and S.B. Bavdekar (2008). "Clinical research in India: Great expectations?", *Journal of Postgraduate Medicine* 54(4): 318.

Turner, J.R. (2002). *The Randomized Clinical Trial.* White Paper. Quintiles.

Wendler, D., E. J. Emanuel and R.K. Lie (2004). "The standard of care debate: can research in developing countries be both ethical and responsive to those countries' health needs?", *American Journal of Public Health* 94(6): 923-28.

Appendices

Appendix I
Registered Ethics Committees in India (State-wise)

S. No.	State	Institutional	Independent	Total
1	Andhra	86	27	113
2	Assam	6	2	8
3	Bihar	5	1	6
4	Chattisgarh	5	0	5
5	Delhi	46	18	64
6	Goa	4	2	6
7	Gujarat	81	43	124
8	Haryana	12	1	13
9	Himachal Pradesh	2	0	2
10	Jammu & Kashmir	2	0	2
11	Karnataka	84	28	112
12	Kerala	52	5	57
13	Madhya Pradesh	13	0	13
14	Maharashtra	184	75	259
15	Mizzoram	1	0	1
16	Orissa	12	0	12
17	Puducherry	7	1	8
18	Punjab	20	1	21
19	Rajasthan	31	4	35
20	Sikkim	1	0	1
21	Tamilnadu	86	25	111
22	Uttrakhand	5	1	6
23	Uttar Pradesh	48	7	55
24	West Bangal	43	2	45
25	Jharkhand	1	0	1
	Total	837	243	1080

Source: Compiled from data on CDSCO, Data as on January 2016.

Appendix II
Causality between Intervention and Injury/Death

According to the ICH Harmonized Tripartite Guideline on Clinical Safety Data Management (E2A), an adverse event is defined as "any untoward medical occurrence in a patient or a clinical investigation subject administered a pharmaceutical product, and which does not necessarily have to have a causal relationship with the treatment". An unexpected adverse drug reaction as an "adverse reaction, the nature or severity of which is not consistent with the applicable product information (e.g., IB for an unapproved investigational medicinal product)". Further, a SAE or Serious ADR is defined as "any untoward medical occurrence that at any dose results in death, is life-threatening, requires inpatient hospitalisation or prolongation of existing hospitalisation, results in persistent or significant disability/incapacity, or results in a congenital anomaly/birth defect".

ADRs are described as one of the frequent causes of morbidity and mortality, in spite of wide-ranging and well-regulated registration practices for verifying drug efficacy and safety. The assessment of adverse events by the investigator and/or sponsor in any clinical trial is done on the basis of the following parameters-

1. Seriousness: As defined by the regulatory authorities.
2. Expectedness: An "unexpected" adverse reaction is one, the nature or severity of which is not consistent with information in the relevant source document(s).
3. Severity: Intensity of a specific event. The grading scale for severity is based on the following: parameters:
   - Study population.
   - Phase of product development (I-IV).
   - Product evaluated (small molecule, therapeutic biologic, device, vaccine).
4. Relatedness/Causality: Causality appraisal is recognised as a vital tool of pharmacovigilance as it evaluates the probability that a detected untoward event is produced by a specific medication. It also diminishes the discrepancy between assessors, categorizes relatedness likelihood, and improves the scientific evaluation of an ADRs.

Methods of Evaluation of Causality

Expert judgment (global introspection): The causality inference is obtained via clinical judgment, such as with an expert panel. It is the most universally used method for individual causality assessment of adverse drug reports, however it is subjective since it essentially mirrors the views of the experts.

Probabilistic methods (Bayesian approaches): This methods uses Bayesian Adverse Reaction Diagnostic Instrument (BARDI) and needs a probability for causality calculated from available knowledge (prior estimate). In addition, it needs specific findings in a case, which combined with the background information, determine the probability of drug causation for the case (posterior estimate). This method is apparently more sensitive, has a positive predictive value and provides the outcome as incessant probabilities. However, it has poor specificity and is practically complex.

Algorithms: These are sets of specific questions which could be either answered by "yes", "no" or "unknown" or for which plus or minus point scores could be given for calculating the likelihood of a cause-effect co-relation. Then, a causality assessment is made by calculating the number of points; depending on the point score, the strength of the causal relationship is considered "definite, probable, possible or unlikely". Some examples of algorithms/scales used for causality assessment are:

- WHO assessment scale.
- Karch and Lasagna's scale.
- Naranjo's scale.
- Kramer scale.
- Yale logarithm.
- European ABO system.
- Spanish imputation system.

These methods have poor sensitivity but good specificity. These improvise the logical feature of causality assessment, although these methods could not ascertain the causality consistently.

The various causality categories as delineated by WHO-Uppsala Monitoring Centre (UMC):

- Certain.
- Probable/Likely.
- Possible.
- Unlikely.
- Conditional/Unclassified.
- Un-assessable/Unclassifiable.

Further, the following information on different aspects while evaluating an ADR is considered:

- Temporal relationship.
- Dose relationship.
- De-challenge (dose reduction)/Re-challenge (dose increase).
- Recognised association with the product/class.
- Pharmacological plausibility.

- Underlying illness/concurrent conditions.
- Other medications.

The Working Group VI on Management of Safety Information from Clinical Trials (2005) of the Council for International Organisations of Medical Sciences (CIOMS) uses a binary yes/no causality assessment. The grades of causality (e.g. 'possible', 'probable', 'definite') do not offer too much practical advantage. Only 'related' versus 'unrelated' is needed for regulatory reporting requirements. Events are considered related if there is "a reasonable possibility of a causal relationship" rather than if "a causal relationship cannot be ruled out.

Causality Assessments by the Regulatory Authorities

1. European Medical Agency (EMA)

In the EU Individual Case Safety Report (ICSR) Implementation Guide, all adverse events judged either by the reporting investigator or the sponsor as having a reasonable causal relationship to the Investigational Medicinal Products (IMP) (and/or concomitant therapy in case of suspicion of interaction with the IMP) should qualify as adverse reactions. It follows the binary decision method detailed in the CIOMS Working Group VI report for each event/reaction reported in the ICSR for causality assessment. Further, the use of other methods of causality assessment is optional and can be provided in accordance with the ICH E2B (R3) Implementation Guide. Any initial ICSR submitted to The EudraVigilance Clinical Trial Module (EVCTM) should contain at least one reaction with a causality assessment of 'reasonable possibility' to at least one of the reported medicinal products classified as suspect or interacting. When the sponsor is sending the report at an early stage and does not have sufficient information to assign causalities between the reported medicinal products classified as suspect or interacting and the reported adverse events/reactions, a 'reasonable possibility' of causal association should be considered until further information is available to confirm or downgrade the initially reported causality.

2. US Food and Drug Authority (USFDA)

In 2010, FDA published a final rule amending the IND safety reporting requirements under 21 CFR part 312 and adding safety reporting requirements for persons conducting BA and BE studies under 21 CFR part 320. According to the document, an adverse event (also referred to as an adverse experience) can be any unfavorable and unintended sign (e.g., an abnormal laboratory finding), symptom, or disease temporally associated with the use of a drug, and does not imply any judgment about causality. An adverse event can arise with any use of the drug (e.g., off-label use, use in combination with another drug) and with any route of administration, formulation, or dose, including an overdose. An adverse reaction means any adverse event caused by a drug. Adverse reactions are a subset of all suspected adverse reactions where there is reason to conclude that the drug caused the event. An adverse event or suspected adverse reaction is considered "unexpected" if it is not listed in the investigator brochure or is not listed at the specificity or severity that has been observed; or, if an investigator brochure is not required or available, is not consistent with the risk information described in the general investigational plan or elsewhere in the current application, as amended. An adverse event or suspected adverse reaction is considered "serious" if, in the view of either the investigator or sponsor, it results in any of the following outcomes: death, a life-threatening adverse event, inpatient hospitalisation or prolongation of existing hospitalisation, a persistent or significant incapacity or substantial disruption of the ability to conduct normal life functions, or a congenital anomaly/birth defect. Following are the various categories of serious adverse events:

Category A: An event that is uncommon and known to be strongly associated with drug exposure.

Category B: An event that is not commonly associated with drug exposure and is uncommon in the population exposed to the drug.

Category C: Events that an aggregate analysis of data from a clinical development programme indicates occur more frequently in the drug treatment group than in a concurrent or historical control.

Under 21 CFR 312.64, investigators are required to provide a causality assessment for each serious adverse event reported to the sponsor. For the purposes of IND safety reporting, 'reasonable possibility' means that there is evidence to suggest a causal relationship between the drug and the adverse event. The sponsor is responsible for making the causality judgment for this rule. For serious events that are unexpected, the sponsor considers the investigator's causality assessment but submits an IND safety report only for those events for which the sponsor determines there is a reasonable possibility that the drug caused the event, regardless of the investigator's causality assessment. The application of the reasonable possibility causality standard is considered to be consistent with the discussion about causality in the ICH E2A guidance.

Compensation for Injury in Drug Trials in India

At present, Schedule Y does not specify the method by which causality assessments are made. The expert committee currently uses a method that has been described as "global introspection" or "the application of collective wisdom of experts". The current compensation rule states that even if an AE was not causally linked to IP, it could be labeled as clinical trial related injury. This could lead to a discrepancy between SAE reporting to Indian regulatory authorities and international regulatory agencies. As per the compensation rule, the EC, the EC and the CDSCO would review the causality assessment made by the investigator and the sponsor. This means the EC, the EC and the CDSCO may not agree with the causality assessment made by the investigator and the sponsor. If the SAE is considered clinical trial related by the investigator and the sponsor, it is likely to remain unchanged. However, if the SAE is not considered clinical trial related by the investigator and sponsor, the EC, the EC and the CDSCO may change the status to clinical trial related. This would have an impact on the overall safety profile of the IP.

Process of causality assessment: The investigator is supposed to forward the SAE reports after due analysis, which would be similar to an SAE case narrative, which is a summary all relevant clinical and related information, including patient characteristics, therapy details, medical history, clinical course of the events, diagnosis and adverse drug reactions including the outcome, laboratory evidence and any other information that supports or refutes a causality assessment.

Seven specific criteria mentioned in the new regulation on compensation enacted by the CDSCO on 30 January 2013, for determining relatedness of injury and death to the trial are the following:

(a) adverse effect of investigational product;

(b) violation of approved protocol, scientific misconduct or negligence by the sponsor or his representative or the investigator;

(c) failure of investigational product to provide intended therapeutic effect;

(d) use of placebo in placebo controlled trial;

(e) adverse effect due to concomitant medication, excluding standard care, necessitated as part of approved protocol;

(f) for injury to a child in-utero because of participation of parent in clinical trial;

(g) any clinical trial procedure in the study.

Formula for calculation of compensation in clinical trials

Drugs Controller General (India) constituted three independent expert committees. The Committee after deliberations prepared a formula to be followed for the determination of quantum of compensation in case of CT related death. The following factors emerged for discussion:

- F1: Age of the subject,
- F2: Risk of death,
- F3: Income of the subject,
- F4: Co-morbidity of the subject at the time of SAE (death),
- F5: Expected survival,
- F6: Dependency on the deceased
- F7: Concomitant medication ,
- F8: Gender of the subject,
- F9: Negligence during the conduct of CT,
- F10: Duration of the disease,
- F11: Industry vs. Academia vs. Institute v/s Sponsor,
- F12: Expectedness of drug to cause death.

Factors finalised for calculation of quantum of compensation

- Age of the subject.
- Risk factor depending on the seriousness and severity of the disease, presence of co-morbidity and duration of disease of the subject at the time of enrolment in the CT, between a scale of 0.5-4:

    - 0.5—Terminally ill patient (expected survival not more than (NMT) 6 months).
    - 1.0—Patient with high risk (expected survival between 6-24 months).
    - 2.0—Patient with moderate risk.
    - 3.0—Patient with mild risk.
    - 4.0—Healthy volunteers or subject of no risk.

Final formula for compensation in case of death

Following three factors will be used for calculation of the quantum of compensation in case of SAE (Death) related to clinical trials are: age, risk and base amount

$$\text{Compensation} = \frac{B * F * R}{99.37}$$

Where, B = Base amount (i.e. 8 lacs); F = Factor depending on the age of the subject as per Annexure 1 (based on Workmen Compensation Act); R = Risk Factor.

Similarly, formulae in case of a SAE causing permanent disability/life threatening illness to the participant or resulting in a congenital anomaly or birth defect, were developed.

Appendix III

Clinical Trial Registries and their Evolution

A clinical trials registry is an official platform and catalogue for registering a clinical trial. It enhances transparency and aids evidence based policies and practices by facilitating accessibility of their information by patients, physicians, researchers and other interested stakeholders. It increases participation in clinical trials and can eliminate publication bias. The International Committee of Medical Journal Editors (ICMJE) requires, and recommends that all medical journal editors require, registration of clinical trials in a public trials registry at or before the time of first patient enrollment as a condition of consideration for publication. The ICMJE accepts registration in any registry that is a primary register of the WHO International Clinical Trials Registry Platform (ICTRP) or in ClinicalTrials.gov, which is a data provider to the WHO ICTRP. An acceptable registry must include the minimum 20-item trial registration dataset at the time of registration and before enrollment of the first participant. A key example is: ClinicalTrials.gov

ClinicalTrials.gov was created as a result of the Food and Drug Administration Modernisation Act of 1997 (FDAMA). FDAMA required the US Department of Health and Human Services, through NIH, to establish a registry of clinical trials information for both federally and privately funded trials conducted under INDA to test the effectiveness of experimental drugs for serious or life-threatening diseases and conditions. NIH and the FDA jointly developed the site, which was made available to the public in February 2000. The ClinicalTrials.gov registration requirements were expanded after Congress passed the FDA Amendments Act of 2007 (FDAAA). The law also requires the submission of results for certain trials. This led to the development of the ClinicalTrials.gov results database. The results database was made available to the public in September 2008.

In November 2014 the US Department of Health and Human Services issued a notice of proposed rulemaking (NPRM) describing the proposed requirements and procedures for registering and submitting the results, including adverse events, of clinical trials on ClinicalTrials.gov, in accordance with FDAAA 801.

In November 2014 NIH proposed a policy to ensure that every clinical trial that receives NIH funding is registered on ClinicalTrials.gov and has summary results submitted and posted in a timely manner, whether subject to FDAAA 801 or not.

In January 2015 the NIH National Cancer Institute (NCI) issued its Policy Ensuring Public Availability of Results from NCI-supported Clinical Trials. Generally, for "all initiated or commenced NCI-Supported Interventional CTs whether extramural or intramural" (i.e., covered trials), "Final Trial Results are expected to be reported in a publicly accessible manner within 12 months of the Trial's Primary Completion Date regardless of whether the clinical trial was completed as planned or terminated earlier."

By September 2016, the final rule mandating registration became part of the federal register. This final rule clarified and expanded requirements for the submission of clinical trial registration and results information to the ClinicalTrials.gov database. The intention was to improve public access to information about certain clinical trials of US.

This web-based resource is maintained by the National Library of Medicine (NLM) at the National Institutes of Health (NIH). Most of the records on ClinicalTrials.gov describe clinical trials (also called interventional studies). It does not contain information about the clinical studies conducted in the US that are not required by law to be registered (for example, observational studies and trials that do not study a drug, biologic, or device). Registration is required for trials that meet the FDAAA 801 definition of an "applicable clinical trial" and were either initiated after September 27, 2007, or initiated on or before that date and were still ongoing as of December 26, 2007. Pediatric post-market surveillance of devices ordered under Section 522 of the Federal Food, Drug, and Cosmetic Act (PDF) as amended by Section 307 of FDAAA are considered and must be registered on ClinicalTrials.gov and have results information submitted.

Evolution of other Clinical Trial Registries

Following the Ministerial Summit on Health Research, in Mexico City, Mexico, in 2004, participants called for the WHO to facilitate the establishment of: "a network of international clinical trials registers to ensure a single point of access and the unambiguous identification of trials". In 2006 the World Health Organisation (WHO) stated that all clinical trials should be registered. The ICTRP was established at the WHO in 2007 to bring together data on trials registered in national and regional registries around the world, thus providing one single point of access to all registered clinical trials globally. In October 2008 the 59th World Medical Association (WMA) General Assembly amended the Declaration of Helsinki - Ethical Principles for Medical Research Involving Human Subjects. Two newly added principles (paragraphs 19 and 30) considered the prospective registration and the public disclosure of study results to be ethical obligations. In October 2013 the European Medicines Agency (EMA) released a new version of the European Clinical Trials Database (EudraCT), marking "the initial step of a process through which summary clinical trial results will be made publicly available through the EU Clinical Trials Register (EU CTR). Other than the national and international registries, there are company registries and associations.

The primary registries in the WHO Registry Network are the national and international registries which meet specific criteria for content, quality and validity, accessibility, unique identification, technical capacity and administration.

Primary registries meet the requirements of the ICMJE. Key examples include:

- Australian New Zealand Clinical Trials Registry (ANZCTR);
- Brazilian Clinical Trials Registry (ReBec);
- Chinese Clinical Trial Registry (ChiCTR);
- Clinical Research Information Service (CRiS), Republic of Korea;
- Clinical Trials Registry-India (CTRI);
- Cuban Public Registry of Clinical Trials(RPCEC);
- EU Clinical Trials Register (EU-CTR);
- German Clinical Trials Register (DRKS);
- Iranian Registry of Clinical Trials (IRCT);
- ISRCTN.org;
- Japan Primary Registries Network (JPRN);
- Thai Clinical Trials Registry (TCTR);
- The Netherlands National Trial Register (NTR);
- Pan African Clinical Trial Registry (PACTR);
- Sri Lanka Clinical Trials Registry (SLCTR) etc.

ICTRP, the WHO registry network provides prospective trial registries with a forum to exchange information and work together to establish best practice for clinical trial registration. The key challenge is in synthesizing information across the ICTRP's numerous registries, due to formatting differences and inconsistencies between registries. A comparison of three registries is given to illustrate the point.

CTRI: It is a free online public record system, launched on 20 July 2007, for registration of CTs conducted in India. Although initiated as a voluntary measure, since 15 June 2009, trial registration in the CTRI has been made mandatory by the DCGI. Today, any researcher who plans to conduct a trial involving human participants, of any intervention such as drugs, surgical procedures, preventive measures, lifestyle modifications, devices, educational or behavioural treatment, rehabilitation strategies as well as trials being conducted in the purview of the Department of AYUSH, is expected to register the trial in the CTRI before enrollment of the first participant. Multi-country trials, where India is a participating country, which have been registered in an international registry, are also expected to be registered in the CTRI. CTRI will also accept registration of trials conducted in other countries in the region, which do not have a primary registry of its own.

However, the CTRI database is so structured that a meta-analysis of the trial entries is virtually impossible. Although every clinical trial entry is rich with significant data, an in-depth trend analysis is not possible. If the intent is to improve public access to information, one of the future challenges would involve restructuring of the CTRI database to make it more user friendly.

EU-CTR: The EU-CTR contains information on interventional clinical trials on medicines that started after 1 May 2004 in the EU, or the EEA.

- CTs conducted outside the EU/EEA are included if:
  - they form part of a PIP, or:
  - they are sponsored by a marketing authorisation holder, and involve the use of a medicine in the paediatric population as part of an EU marketing authorisation.

The register also provides information about older paediatric trials covered by an EU marketing authorisation. The register enables search for information in the EudraCT database. The EMA imposed a mandatory requirement on 14 July 2014 for sponsors to post clinical trial results in EudraCT.

ISRCTN.org: is a registry and curated database containing the basic set of data items, essential to describe a study at inception, as per the requirements set out by the WHO ICTRP and the ICMJE guidelines. It is owned by ISRCTN—a not-for-profit organisation. All study records in the database are freely accessible and searchable and have been assigned an ISRCTN ID. The ISRCTN Register is managed by Current Controlled Trials Ltd, which is part of a scientific publishing group. The registry launched in 2000, originally stood for 'International Standard Randomised Controlled Trial Number'; however, over the years the scope of the registry has widened to observational and interventional trials.

Challenges Faced by Clinical Trial Registries

1. Lack of harmonisation and reliability of data quality across registries. Such harmonisation would avoid inadvertent duplicate registrations, ensure that interventions have unambiguous names, and have a search engine that identifies all trials that meet a user's specifications.

2. Data quality: Contrary to ICMJE guideline that on "trial registration with missing or uninformative fields for the minimum data elements is inadequate", many registered records of clinical trials are currently incomplete, not accurate, not up-to-date or are retrospectively registered.

3. (In)accessibility of protocols, results and participant-level data: To address the lack of availability of trial results countries, such as the USA, EU, Canada and Japan, as well as the WHO have implemented measures. In contrast to CSRs, publicly available sources like journal publications and registry reports provide insufficient information on patient-relevant outcomes of clinical trials or even for published trials. In June 2013, the EMAreleased a draft policy calling for the proactive publication of complete clinical trial data (possibly including CSRs). In addition, the EU and the European Commission are considering legal

measures to improve the transparency of clinical trial data. In 2014, NPRM proposed regulations for submitting clinical trial registration and summary results information to ClinicalTrials.gov, regardless of whether the drugs, biological products, or devices under study have been approved, licensed, or cleared for marketing by the FDA. The measures remain to be widely implemented in many other countries where less progress has been made towards sharing of participant-level data sets.

4. Searchability, data aggregation and linking at the ICTRP and registries: ICTRP's search interface lags behind the interfaces of major bibliographic databases. Providing opportunities for aggregate analyses is another area of improvement for the ICTRP. Currently, lack of fields for links with ICTRP, to all related documents and data for each clinical trials is another drawback. The search function quality, aggregate analysis possibilities and provision of links vary greatly per registry.

Appendix IV
Snapshot of Country wise Regulations and Field Findings

Characteristic	India	USA	South Africa	UK	Germany	Singapore	Indonesia
National Drug Regulatory Authority	CDSCO	USFDA	MCC	MHRA	BfArM	HSA	BPOM
No of Registered Ethics Committees	1080	4789	44	>80	53	Data not available	Data not available
Approval Timelines (Normative)	>12 weeks	~4 weeks	>12 weeks	~4 weeks	~4 weeks	~4 weeks; 5 working days for notification	>12 weeks
Ethical Review Process & NDRA Review	Parallel Authorisation	Parallel Authorisation	Parallel Authorisation	Parallel Authorisation	Parallel Authorisation	Parallel for Authorisation; Serial for notification	Serial Authorisation
CT application	No Objection Certificate (NOC)	Authorisation (Application deemed approved if no reply received from NDRA)	Authorisation	Authorisation (Application deemed approved if no reply received from NDRA)	Authorisation (Application deemed approved if no reply received from NDRA)	Authorisation and Notification for Minimal Risk Trials	Authorisation
Clinical Trial Registry	CTRI	Clinicaltrials.gov	SANCTR	EUCTR	DRKS	HSACTR	INA Registry
Compensation Norms for Injury or Death	Formula Based; Quantum of Compensation is fixed - Based on the age of the subject, a minimum and maximum amount is arrived after causality is fixed.	No Formula; No FDA regulation; Institutional policies decide if compensation is to be paid; Tort Laws for claims	No Formula; ABPI Compensation Guidelines	No Regulations; ABPI Guidelines on Compensation; Typically No Fault Insurance	No formula; Verschuldensunabhängig Provisions; The maximum insurance sum per person for each case of death or permanent disability is at least 500 000 per person	No formula; ABPI Compensation Guidelines; No Specific Guideline by HSA, but adopts Medicines Act Chapter 176	No formula; Standard Indemnity Insurance
Role of Commercial/ Independent Ethics Committees (Non-institutional)	Allowed to review only BA/BE protocols	Full Review	Full Review	Full Review	Full Review	Full Review	Full Review
Audio Visual Recording of IC Process	Yes, for vulnerable population/groups in NCE/GCT trials	No AV recording	No AV recording	No AV recording	No AV recording	No AV recording	No AV recording
EC Registration	Centralised and Mandatory	Centralised and Mandatory	Centralised and Mandatory	Centralised and Mandatory	Centralised and Mandatory	Centralised and Mandatory	Centralised and Mandatory

Source: Author's compilation from field file.

Appendix V

The Swasthya Adhikar Manch & Others Vs Union of India: A Timeline

Following several media reports of unethical conduct of CTs in India, Swasthya Adhikar Manch,[1] an NGO filed a public interest litigation alleging malpractices in clinical trials conducted in India. Interim orders passed in the said PIL led to frequency changes and brought unpredictability in the existing regulations pertaining to Clinical trials.

Below is the chronology of the orders passed by the Hon'ble Supreme Court of India in the said case:[2]

8th October, 2012

On this date of hearing, the Hon'ble Supreme Court sought clarifications from Ministry of Health and Family Welfare, Government of India and/or Central Drugs Standard Control Organisation on various issues such as:

i) The number of experimental New Clinical Entities (NCEs) approved for clinical trials by the Drug Controller General of India (DCGI) from January 1, 2005 to June 30, 2012.

ii) Whether deaths were suffered by subjects of clinical trials. If yes, the number of deaths.

iii) Whether serious side effects were suffered by the subjects of clinical trials. If yes, the number of such subjects and the nature of side effects, and

iv) The details of compensation paid to the subjects who suffered side effects or paid to the family of the subjects who suffered death.

3 January 2013

On this date of hearing, the reply submitted by the Ministry did not satisfy the Supreme Court and the Court granted more time to the central ministry to comply with the earlier order. On this date of hearing, the court was assured that until any further order by it, CTs of a NCE would only be conducted strictly in accordance with the procedure prescribed in Schedule 'Y' of Drugs & Cosmetics Act, 1940 and under the direct supervision of the Secretary, Ministry of Health & Family Welfare.

26 July 2013

The Government of India submitted its reply to the questions put up by the judges. To comply with the directions of the Supreme Court and to strengthen the existing regulatory framework, the existing gazette notifications G.S.R. 53(E) dated 30.01.2013, G.S.R. 63(E) dated 01.02.2013 and G.S.R. No.72E dated 08.02.2013 were amended. GS.R. 53(E) specifies the procedure to analyse the reports of serious adverse events including deaths occurring during CTs and procedures for the payment of compensation in case of trial related injury or death. G.S.R. 63(E) specifies various conditions for conduct of clinical trials, authority to conduct CT inspections and actions in case of non-compliance. G.S.R. 72(E) provides for requirements and guidelines for registration of EC. By amendment, it was proposed that no EC can review and approve any clinical trial protocol unless it is registered with the CDSCO and that in case of non-compliance, the registration can be suspended/cancelled.

30 September 2013

It was submitted in the Court that the Ministry of Health & Family Welfare convened a meeting with various state governments which were duly considered and the ministry made the following observations:

a. Even though concerns have been raised about the conduct of clinical trials in the country, clinical trials are necessary for the development of new drugs in the country. India has the capacity and knowhow for drug discovery research. However, there should be a robust system for conducting clinical trials in the country to ensure that trials are conducted in a scientific and ethical manner and in compliance to the regulatory provisions.

b. Restricting clinical trials to Government Hospitals alone would not provide a solution. What is required is a robust system for regulating the conduct of clinical trials in the country.

c. The amount of money paid by the sponsor/companies to the investigator for conduct of clinical trial may act as an inducement to the investigator for conducting clinical trials. Sometimes such inducement may lead to bias in enrolment of subjects in the trials.

d. Regulatory provisions may be made so that information relating to the amount of money paid by the companies to investigators for conduct of clinical trials is in the knowledge of the regulatory authorities.

e. There are some concerns on certain clauses of the amendment of Drugs & Cosmetics Rules made on 30.1.2013 regarding compensation in clinical trials. Some amendments in these clauses may be required.

f. A Committee constituted under the chairmanship of Dr. Ranjit Roy Chaudhury for formulating guidelines on clinical trials and new drugs has submitted its report. The report will be helpful in further strengthening of the regulation of CTs in the country.

---

1. Swasthya Adhikar Manch Vs Union of India [Writ Petition (Civil) 33 of 2012]
2. Supreme Court Orders as available on the official website of Supreme Court of India *www.supremecourtofindia.nic*. Last visited on 18 March 2016.

g. States' suggestions and views would be considered for further strengthening of the regulation of clinical trial.

The Court was further informed that 577 clinical trial sites were inspected and notices were issued to the investigators/sponsors/ethics committees seeking clarifications in 235 cases. It was also submitted that a system of supervision of clinical trials of new chemical entities by constituting apex committee and technical committee had been put in place. The government submitted that until 31 August 2013, 12 NDACs have met 78 times and evaluated a total number of 1,122 applications for approval of clinical trials, new drugs and fixed dose combinations. Out of these 1,122 applications, 331 were related to approval of GCT including clinical trials of new chemical entities. Of these 331 GCT applications, NDACs after deliberations recommended 285 applications for approval. For 46 applications, no recommendation had been made. Out of above 285 applications, DCG (I) had given approval to conduct CTs in 162 cases until 31 August 2013.

21 October 2013

The Supreme Court passed the said dated order only with respect to the 162 cases which were granted approval by DCG (I) until 31 August 2013. Of these, 157 approvals were given by the DCG (I) before 31 December 2012 which were prior to the directions of the Supreme Court on 03 March 2013. The DCG (I) gave the approval to conduct clinical trials in the remaining 5 cases from 01 January 2013 until 31 August 2013 after the approval of the Apex Committee assisted by the Technical Committee. It was stated that these 5 cases had undergone the three-tier screening—first by the NDACs, then by the Technical Committee and the Apex Committee and thereafter by the DCG (I). It was also submitted in the Court that the 157 approvals which were given by the DCG(I) before 03 January 2013, were not evaluated by the Technical Committee and the Apex Committee. It was submitted by the central government that the 157 cases may be evaluated by the Technical Committee and the Apex committee as well, as had been done for the 5 cases for which approval was given after 03 January 2013.

The Supreme Court while accepting this statement of the central government was of the view that the Technical committee and the Apex Committee while evaluating the 157 cases had to keep in view all relevant aspects of safety and efficacy particularly in terms of assessment of risk versus benefit to the patients, innovation vis-a-vis existing therapeutic options and the unmet medical need in the country.

While refusing to pass any order with respect to the 157 cases, the Supreme Court accepted the assurance of the central government that CTs in respect of 5 cases, for which approvals have been given, would commence after a proper framework was in place concerning audio-visual recording of the informed concerned process and the preservation of documents while adhering to the principles of confidentiality.

10 March 2014

The petitioners in the case alleged before the court that as regards approval of 475 trials including NCEs from January 2005 to June 2012, 506 subjects had suffered serious adverse effects arising from clinical trials conducted during the period and no compensation had been paid to or provided for the subjects. The Supreme Court of India directed the central ministry to furnish the information about the number of deaths/injury of subjects which were due to clinical trials that were granted approval of NCEs.

21 April 2014

The Supreme Court directed that to avoid any future controversy, three specific columns regarding certain parameters are to be inserted while seeking information from the applicants for NCEs/GCTs. These three parameters are: (i) assessment of risk versus benefit to the patients, (ii) innovation vis-a-vis existing therapeutic option and (iii) unmet medical need in the country.

5 January 2017

On this date of hearing, the parties present before the court i.e. the petitioners as well as all the States were asked to file their comments as well as any new additional developments which have occurred during the last two years in the form of an affidavit before the Court.

10 February 2017 and 23 March 2017

On both these dates, the case was adjourned for further dates. Now the case is likely to be listed on 19 July 2017.

Appendix VI
Schematic Diagram of Review Process of Clinical Trial Application in India

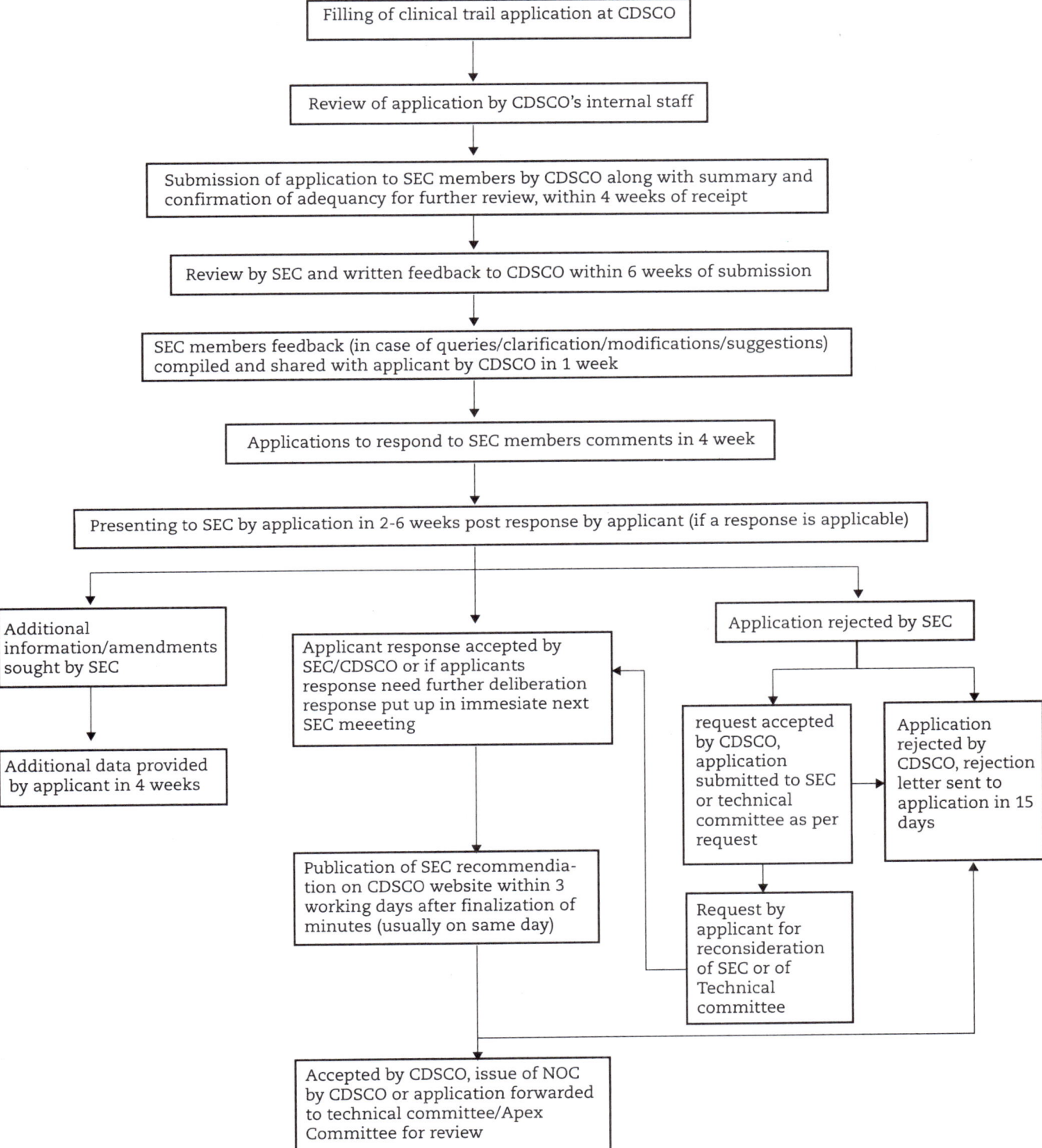

Source: Adapted from 'Handbook for applicants and reviewers of clinical trials of new drugs in India, January, 2017.

Appendix VII

Timeline of Changes in Regulation from 2013 to Till Date

S. No	Date	Order No	Major Changes
1.	2013	Order	Order passed by the office of Drugs Controller General (India) laying down the system of prescreening for submission of reports of SAEs to CDSCO.*
2.	30.01.2013	GSR 53(E)	Insertion of Rule 122-DAB: Sponsor of clinical trial made liable for compensation in case of injury or death related to trial. Appendix XII was inserted which talked about and described the process compensation in case of injury or death during a trial.
3.	01.02.2013	GSR 63 (E)	Insertion of Rule 122 DAC: Listed down conditions before permission to conduct clinical trial is given. This Rule also states the repercussions in case of non-compliance of any of the conditions laid down.
4.	06.02.2013	Order	Order passed by MOHFW constituting two expert committees to formulate policy guidelines and SOPs for approval of new drugs, clinical trials, banning of drugs and FDCs. In a separate order the Ministry constituted two committees i.e. Apex Committee and a Technical Committee as per the directions of the Supreme Court for supervision and monitoring of clinical trials in India.
5.	08.02.2013	GSR 72 (E)	Insertion of Rule 122 DD: Registration of Ethics Committee(s) made mandatory. Provision for inspection of ECs by the CDSCO or SDRA.
6.	19.03.2013		Three independent expert committees were constituted to examine the SAE reports of deaths being occurred during a clinical trial.
7.	07.06.2013	GSR 364 (E)	Insertion of mandatory Audio Visual consent as a part of the Informed Consent Process in Schedule Y.
8.	10.09.2013		CDSCO came out with a compensation formula to determine the quantum of compensation in cases of trial related SAEs of deaths during CT. **
9.	19.11.2013	Administrative Order	Audio video recording of the informed consent process made mandatory in addition to the written informed consent.
10.	10.12.2013	Order	Inclusion of at least two government hospitals or medical colleges/institutions as sites made mandatory
11.	09.01.2014		Draft guidelines on AV recording of the Informed Consent Process in Clinical trial were formulated by the CDSCO and invited comments.
12.	07.04.2014		A checklist of system of pre-Screening for submission of reports of SAEs to CDSCO was released. Some changes such as causality assessment to be provided along with reasoning, copy of the Informed Consent Form signed by parties etc
13.	22.04.2014		The above checklist was revised again.
14.	24.04.2014	GSR 292 (E)	Ministry of Health published Draft Rules called the Drugs and Cosmetics (Third Amendment) Rules 2014. Rule 122-DAB amended to include free medical management as long as required or till such time it is established that the injury is not related to the clinical trial.
15.	01.05.2014		CDSCO came out with a draft formula to determine quantum of compensation in Clinical Trial related serious adverse events (SAES) of deaths occurring during CTs.***

* http://www.cdsco.nic.in/writereaddata/System%20of%20Pre-screening%20for%20submission%20of%20reports%20of%20SAEs%20to%20CDSCO.pdf
** http://www.cdsco.nic.in/writereaddata/formula2013SAE.pdf
*** http://www.cdsco.nic.in/writereaddata/formula2013SAE.pdf

16.	3.07.2014	Orders	DCGI came out with a series of orders. These are as follows:
			Drugs that are considered generics and similar biologics (biosimilars) in other countries like USA that have been marketed in such countries for more than four years and have a satisfactory report would be approved for marketing in India after abbreviated trials.
			If India participates in global clinical trial of NCEs to be used for diseases that are prevalent in Indian population, approval should be sought from CDSCO for marketing these NCEs in India after approval of the drug in the innovator country or in well-regulated developed country markets, After approval from CDSCO, these NCEs should be marketed in India, speedily, preferably by production within the country.
			Requirement regarding placebo controlled trial: The Sponsor/ CRO/Clinical Trial Applicants/ Ethics Committees/Investigators are required to ensure that the design used in a placebo controlled clinical trial is appropriate, efficient and ethical. The NDAC (SEC) members are also requested to ensure that only those placebo controlled trials, design of which are appropriate, efficient and ethical, are considered for approval.
			Requirement of considering ethnicity for approval of new drugs. The order states various properties of a compound which make it more likely to be sensitive to ethnic factors. The order also lists various factors to be considered before it is decided whether the available data is ethnically sensitive or not.
			Requirement stating that waiver of clinical trial in Indian population for approval of new drugs, which have already been approved outside India, can presently be considered only in cases of national emergency, extreme urgency, and epidemic and for orphan drugs for rare diseases and drugs indicated for conditions/diseases for which there is no therapy
			New Drug Advisory Committee was renamed as Subject Expert Committees.
			The order states that the sponsor/applicant has to provide compensation to the trial participant/nominee, if any drug-related anomaly is discerned (detected) at a later stage and accepted to be drug related injury or death
			Requirement of a provision for providing ancillary care to the patient suffering from any other illness during the trial. Sponsors/applicants are advised that such ancillary care should be provided to the clinical trial subject for brief illness in the same hospital/trial site, wherever required.
			Requirement that number of clinical trials an investigator can undertake should not be more than three at a time. The responsibility to ensure this rests with Sponsor/applicant. (It is now the responsibility of the EC to ensure this).
			Requirement that NDAC (SEC) experts have to evaluate whether the number of Indian subjects in global clinical trials are adequate, while considering approval of the new drug in India
			The order says that procedures for the clinical trials with medical devices such as approval, accreditations of Investigators, sites, EC and such other conditions would be similar to the clinical trials of new drugs/vaccines.
17.	05.09.2014	Order	Office order relied on the order dated 21.10.2013 passed by the Supreme Court of India and stated that all application for the conduct of Clinical Trials of new drugs in India should provide the following information:
			Assessment of risk versus benefits to the patients
			Innovation vis-a-vis existing therapeutic option
			Unmet medical need in the country
18.	12.12.2014	GSR 889 (E)	Rule 122 DAB amended to state that in case there is no permanent injury, the quantum of compensation shall be commensurate with the nature of non-permanent injury and loss of wages of the subject.
			It was also added that in case standard care has not been provided despite being available and there has been a failure of the product to provide the intended therapeutic effect, compensation will have to be paid incase of injury or death.
			It was also stated that compensation will also be paid in use of placebo in a placebo controlled trial where the standard care was available and still not provided to the subject as per the protocol.
19.	15.12.2014	Order	CDSCO came out with a formulae to determine the quantum of compensation in case of clinical trial related injury (other than death)

20.	24.12.2014	Order	Ministry of Health by an office order constituted a committee to examine and recommend amendments in Drugs and Cosmetics Rules, 1945.
21.	31.07.2015	GSR 611 (E)	Amendments in Schedule Y relating to Informed Consent were made. It was stated that an AV recording of the informed consent process in case of vulnerable subjects in CTs has to be maintained by the investigator.
22.	30.10.2015	GSR 826 (E)	In Rule 122 DA definitions of Clinical Trial, Global clinical trial, Investigational New Drug, New Chemical Entity were added.
23.	29.12.2015	GSR 1011 (E)	Draft rules were published revising regulatory fees
24.	08.03.2016	GSR 287 (E)	It was stated that the applicant shall have a pharmacovigilance system in place for collecting, processing and forwarding the report to the licensing authority for information on adverse drug reactions emerging from the use of the drug manufactured or marketed by the applicant in the country.
25.	16.03.2016	GSR 313 (E)	An academic trial now does not need permission to conduct Clinical Trial in respect of approved drug formulation for any new indication if the trial is approved by the Ethics Committee and the data generated is not intended for submission to the licensing authority. The Ethics committee has to inform the licensing authority about the trials approved and about cases where there could be possible overlap between an academic trial or a trial for regulatory purposes.
26.	13.07.2016	Notice	Notice by DCGI stating that the applicants have to respond to queries posed by the Department within 45 days of seeking the information. If the applicant does not seek extension of time nor replies to the queries, it will be assumed that the applicant is not interested in pursuing and the same would be disposed off on merit. It was also stated that if the application is not disposed off within 2/3rd of the time lines specified, the applicants could seek an appointment with the Joint Drug Controller or the Drug Controller General (India).
27.	02.08.2016	Circulars	CDSCO came out with the following circulars: The restriction regarding conduct of 3 clinical trials per investigator was removed. It was decided that the EC will examine the risk involved and shall decide how many trials an investigator can undertake. The condition that a CT cannot be conducted at a hospital having less than 50 beds was revised. The EC will examine and decide whether a site is suitable for trial or not irrespective of the number of beds.
28.	03.08.2016	Circular	CDSCO came out with a circular stating that the earlier requirement of NOC from DCGI for addition of a new CT site or an investigator in the CT was revised. It is now decided that the respective EC after due diligence can approve the proposals for additional sites and investigators and NOC was not required.
29.	02.12.2016	Circular	CDSCO has issued a notice on 02 Dec 2016 asking feedback from stakeholders on: Processing and approval of applications through online system i.e. SUGAM; Risk based inspections started in the country; NRA assessment through WHO Skill development exercise started by CDSCO DCG(I) Cell for addressing Grievance/Complaints; Amendments in D&C Act & Rules.
30.	13.12.2016	Circular	As per this circular, the timeline for communication of recommendation of Committees to the stakeholders shall not be later than 05 working days.